SING YOUR
NAME OUT
LOUD

SING YOUR NAME OUT LOUD

15 RULES FOR LIVING YOUR DREAM

JASON DERULO

HarperOne

An Imprint of HarperCollinsPublishers

HarperCollins books may be purchased for educational, business, or sales promotional use. For information, please email the Special Markets Department at SPsales@harpercollins.com.

FIRST EDITION

Designed by THE COSMIC LION

Library of Congress Cataloging-in-Publication Data is available upon request.

ISBN 978-0-06-327083-1

23 24 25 26 27 LBC 5 4 3 2 1

To my dear mother,
who taught me the meaning of hard work.
And to my dad for leading by example, showing me
strength, patience, and how to be a man.
I love you both with all my heart.

And to my firstborn son,
may this book help you on your quest
for greatness. The joy is in the journey,
not the destination.

CONTENTS

CONTENTS

AUTHOR NOTE:
SING YOUR NAME OUT LOUD.

One day when I was a kid, maybe around nine years old, my mom came into my bedroom. I won't lie, it was a mess. It always was. My bed wasn't made, and I had laundry scattered everywhere. As a kid, I was always taking clothes from my older brother, Joey. He had nicer clothes than I did, and unlike mine, they were always hung up or neatly folded.

I didn't care then, and I don't care now. A little chaos and disorganization has never bothered me, especially at that point, when I had zero time for cleaning and straightening. I was too busy singing and writing songs and perfecting my craft to notice those things.

My mom has always supported me in everything I've done, but she still couldn't stand the sight of my room. "Jason," she said, "you have to straighten up your room! If you don't learn how to keep things organized, your house will be a mess one day."

I looked at her. "Ma," I said, dead serious, "I'm never going to clean my own house. I'll hire people for that."

From the look on my mom's face, I knew right away that I had said the wrong thing. She looked like she wanted to slap the taste out of my mouth. Of course, looking back on that moment today, I understand why she was instantly angry. I certainly wouldn't word it this way as an adult, but as a kid, this was the only vocabulary I had for what I was feeling. I only said it because I believed it, deeply. What I was trying to say was that I intended to dedicate all of my energy and time toward music, and I knew, in the depths of my heart and without a shadow of a doubt, that I would create a life for myself that allowed me to do just that, forever.

It wasn't just about cleaning. I felt this way about everything else that I was meant to learn or do in those years. When my dad was outside fixing the car, he'd call my brother and me out to join him. Honestly, my brother was happy to learn. I wasn't much help, as I would be singing the song I was working on at the top of my lungs the whole time. Eventually, my dad would let me go back inside to finish the song I was writing that day. Needless to say, my skills around fixing anything in a car are zero today. I had a one-track mind, and still do. Everything else could wait. I was going to be a successful singer, and that was that.

And here's the thing: if I hadn't believed it that deeply and was too afraid to speak it, there's no way that truth would have become a reality.

My mom may have been mad at me for refusing to clean my room, but the truth is that she's the one who taught me how powerful my words are. When I was little, she used to say things like, "Oh, that cheesecake is to die for." But the Bible says, "Death and life are in the power of the tongue." My mom caught on to this, and she started flipping the script. Instead of "to die for," she started to say, "That cheesecake is to *live* for."

As I got older, I made sure to speak out loud about the things I wanted and believed in. I've been saying that I was going to be known all over the world for my music ever since I was four years old. People thought it was cute when I was little, but the older I got, the more pompous and arrogant it sounded. I never meant it that way. My words just reflected the level to which I believed what I was saying.

I never hesitated to speak my truth. When I was eleven, I started saying that I was going to be famous by the time I was twelve. When I was twelve, I said that I was going to be famous by the time I was thirteen. In my mind, this was my reality.

Here's the important thing, though. It was that belief that allowed me to take the necessary steps to get there. I fully believe in the power of manifestation and speaking words into reality, but you can't manifest a dream by saying that something is going to happen and then sitting back and waiting. You need to believe that you can achieve something in your heart of hearts and be willing to put in the necessary work to make it happen.

When you do this, you'll begin to see signs that you're on the right path. It happens slow, and then, all of a sudden, it happens fast. At least, that's how it was for me.

Very early in my career, someone asked me in an interview what artist I would want to tour with if I could choose any artist in the world and I said "Lady Gaga." I ended up touring with Gaga before my first album even came out. I spoke it into existence. A few years ago, I heard that Wiz Khalifa made twenty million in a year, and I said, "Next year, I'm gonna make twenty million, too." That was my mindset. I believed it, and I put in the work to make it happen. That is the power of the spoken word.

The external world believes what you tell it, and your body believes it, too. I used to say things like, "Oh, I'm so blind, I can barely see." I noticed that my vision started to get worse and worse. I used to tell people that I had trouble remembering things, and my memory started to deteriorate, too.

This has gotten more and more intense as the years have gone by, and I've become really careful about what I say. Now you'll never catch me talking bad about myself because I refuse to tell the trillions of cells in my body that I am inadequate in any way, shape, or form. I focus completely on the positive instead.

Nobody teaches us about the power of our thoughts and words, and that's why so few people know this power and trust in it. In school, we're told to fit the mold, to wait in line, and to raise our hands when it's time to speak. We're basically taught how to be timid and to color within the lines instead of how to dream big and make great things happen for ourselves. So, when someone like me says, "I'm going to be the biggest pop star in the world," people think I'm egotistical. They just do not see the world the same way I do.

Just recently, I told my dad that my goal was to be worth five hundred million dollars two years from now and he laughed. But I wasn't playing. "No, Dad, I'm serious," I told him.

Likewise, if I told you that lately my mind has shifted to the fact that there are only seven Black billionaires in this country and that I want to be the eighth, to show Black kids out there that they can use their minds to become successful, you'd probably roll your eyes a little bit. But why? Why not me? Why not *you*? Why does someone else deserve it but not you? Why shouldn't we all dream big, aim high, and believe completely in our ability to succeed?

I hope that reading this book helps you believe in yourself and gives you the confidence that you have all the tools you need to succeed in whatever field and at whatever scale you dream about. I hope my words resonate with you. In addition, I have asked some of my famous friends to offer their own words of advice for living their dreams, and you will find those original quotes at the start of many chapters in this book. Now it's your turn. I want you to remember that whatever you want in this world is within your reach. I know deep in my heart that this is the truth. All you have to do is believe it, speak it, and work your ass off in order to get it. Use your words, your voice, and all of the tools you've got to make it happen for yourself.

AUTHOR NOTE: SING YOUR NAME OUT LOUD.

Here's the beautiful thing: you can start today. We are not slaves to our past. Every day is a fresh start, and we can start our new legacy right this moment. Start now. Sing your name out loud, and let it ring out around the world. I have no doubt that the sound of whatever you want to hear most will echo right back to you.

SING YOUR
NAME OUT
LOUD

YOUR DREAM IS WITHIN YOUR REACH.

My day started at 4:00 a.m., when the clock radio on my nightstand jolted my fourteen-year-old body awake. I had been up late the night before practicing my vocals, and every cell in my body was screaming for more sleep. But I jumped out of bed and did not hit snooze. I never do.

My family's house was small, and I had to be careful not to wake anyone else up as I tiptoed out of my bedroom and into the hallway. First, I hit the bathroom, where I changed into my clothes for the day. I usually wore baggy jeans and a white T-shirt that I'd borrowed (okay, stolen) from my older brother, Joey. Then, I grabbed my book bag and something to eat on the bus, laced up my red and white Sauconys, and raced out of the house and into the warm, early morning southern Florida air.

My house was in a big development, located about thirty minutes outside of Miami, that was filled with families like ours: hardworking immigrants who were trying to make their way. Many of them were my own extended family members. I couldn't throw a penny without hitting an uncle or an auntie or a cousin or two. But no one else—and I mean *no one*—was awake at 4:00 a.m. Not even the newspaper delivery kids or the partygoers from the night before. The sky was still dark, and I was alone.

I loved that walk to the bus stop. The whole world was asleep, and I imagined my surroundings as the backdrop to a music video as

I sang and danced my way through the long, winding development. It was another fifteen minutes around a pond to the basketball court. On the weekends, that court was my second home. If I wasn't in my room singing, you could find me hooping with my boys down at that court. But during the week, I walked right past the court to the bus stop. There was no one there, either. I was the only kid getting on the bus this early to go to school.

Despite my early wake-ups, I still somehow managed to miss the bus at least once a week. Then I'd walk all the way back home and beg my mom or my brother to drive me to school. Eventually, one of them would agree and then spend the entire car ride cussing at me. If I hadn't already been motivated to make the bus, avoiding that car ride would have been all the motivation I needed. Now you know why I never hit snooze!

It was much better for everyone when I made the bus on time and got to spend those ninety minutes thinking about lyrics instead of listening to my family member's grumbling. On that bus ride, I stared out of the window without seeing anything. I was completely lost in my head. Slowly, as the miles ticked by, rough song concepts started to come together. Unbeknownst to me, my thumbs tapped the denim on my thighs, creating an unformed beat.

Finally, I arrived at my performing arts high school, and it was time for the day to officially begin.

When I was in school, I was competitive, intense, and unafraid, with a confidence that I hadn't yet earned. At the same time, I was introverted. It took me a long time to warm up and get to know people. More than anything, I was focused. I worked hard and never complained, and I took every lesson and opportunity that came my way.

I tried to be friendly to everyone and was generally well-liked, but I didn't put much of a focus on my social life. I couldn't ignore the nagging sensation that I had a job to prepare for. I couldn't let myself be distracted by friends. I never went to proms or homecomings or anything like that. I knew deep down that I needed to work hard so I'd be ready when my time came.

Apologies to any of my former teachers who are reading this, but I didn't spend a whole lot of time in class listening to what they had to say. Instead, I worked on my songs. I started with the easy part, the lyrics. I would think about a girl I had noticed in school or a romantic situation that my brother or one of my older cousins had described to me. These were usually scenarios that I hadn't experienced myself and didn't even fully understand yet—falling head over heels for someone, unrequited love, wanting a girl who was impossible to get or to impress, or being caught cheating or being cheated on— but I could always find the words to capture the situation as if it had happened to me.

From a young age, I had an uncanny ability to translate emotions into lyrics, whether or not I had experienced the emotion for myself. I could come up with catchy hooks on the fly and create metaphors out of nothing, but my specialty was always taking a simple and relatable feeling and then putting my signature upbeat and lighthearted twist on it. Writing songs seemed to be in my blood, and I strengthened that DNA with daily practice.

Once I had the lyrics in place, I would come up with a beat or a melody. I had learned to write and read music in elementary school, which made this part much easier than it would have been otherwise. When the song was complete, that would be the end of the project. There was nowhere to upload or share it the way there is now. Every song I wrote ended in the same place it began—in my head.

That didn't matter to me. My job as I saw it was to put in the time. With hours came growth, and I put in a *lot* of them hours. I didn't know exactly what I was working toward, but I had a deep and unwavering knowing that it was going to be something big.

> I didn't know exactly what I was working toward, but I had a deep and unwavering knowing that it was going to be something big.

After school was done in the afternoon, I went to basketball practice. Then, not wanting to get my butt whooped again by my mom or Joey, I often sprinted to catch the last bus home. After another productive ninety-minute ride, I walked through my front door, physically exhausted and mentally spent.

Oh, you thought the day was over, huh?

After a full day of bus rides, school, songwriting, and basketball, pretty much all of the other kids my age were doing normal stuff like playing video games. I wasn't doing any of that. I was singing. While I was naturally good at writing melodies and pairing lyrics with music, my greatest aspiration was always, always to sing.

I knew that to make it as a singer I was going to have to beat all imaginable odds. My biggest critics and my greatest cheerleaders (looking at you, Ma!) all told me as much, and they were right. There were endless barriers keeping a kid like me from becoming a singer. Hell, when I told people that I wanted to be a pop star, most of them straight up laughed at me. That's how unlikely it was. So, if I was going to do this, I couldn't leave anything to chance.

Picture the longest traffic jam you've ever seen in your life. Now multiply it by a thousand. Well, that's nothing compared to the road I was on if I wanted to become a professional singer.

This traffic jam was by design. There were millions of kids out there like me who wanted to sing, record music, and become a star. But there were only so many slots on the radio, MTV, and VH1 (the primary platforms for distributing music at that time). Your chances of selling songs on iTunes depended on your being one of the few artists to somehow get attention from listeners.

But before you could even try to do any of that, you needed a record label. In order for a record label to notice you, you had to get a demo tape together, make sure it was lit, and then get it into the right hands. You had to have a certain "look" that the label could bank on. You had to already have some level of credibility, professional training, and experience, but how were you supposed to get that with all the barriers in your way? Almost every aspiring singer ended up getting caught in that hamster wheel and never making it out.

Of course, it helped if your parents had a bunch of money or knew someone who knew someone who could make a call and put in a good word for you. My parents had little money and had never met anyone who had worked in the music or entertainment industries. So, that was a nonstarter.

But the number one most important thing that you needed to be a singer above anything else was to be great. Undeniable. Elite. In fact, none of that other stuff mattered one bit if you weren't truly exceptional. That's still true.

To reach that level of proficiency required the kind of practice an aspiring professional athlete has to put in. But there are, what, hundreds or thousands of players in the NBA and NFL? Becoming one of them was hard enough. Meanwhile, maybe a few dozen singers would emerge from my generation and have any kind of sustained success, and that's being generous.

To win at singing I would have to be unbeatable whenever a microphone was in my hands. That takes some serious work. I'm talking about a Tiger Woods level of conditioning and training. Hours and hours and hours. No breaks. No days off. Singing the same songs over and over, and noticing every detail of what was working and what wasn't, what notes were a struggle and where I sounded best.

So, every night after school I started working on my craft, on my dream. I don't know how my family could stand it. They must have somehow become deaf to the sounds of me singing "Ben" or "Billie Jean" by Michael Jackson a hundred times each night. Or maybe they were walking around with earplugs in and I never noticed.

But this was nothing new. I had been going like this ever since I'd started elementary school. Probably even longer than that. For all of those years, I had been writing multiple songs and practicing for hours every day. *Every* day.

Where did all that hard work get me? Before I graduated from high school, I had collaborated on songs with Pitbull and Birdman and even worked with P. Diddy. As my second year of college was nearing an end, I had won big-name singing competitions, had hundreds of songs under my belt, and was about to sign a contract with Beluga Heights under a major record label. My first single debuted at the number one spot on the Billboard Top 40, and the next two were also top-ten hits.

And that's when the real work began.

« »

While my first dream has always been singing, and I never stopped training to be my best, I later put my same work ethic toward mastering dancing, then performing, then directing music videos, then creating multiple businesses, and finally diving into social media. At each turn, I relied on a set of principles that I had created during my childhood and teenage years, when I was ferocious, relentless, and determined to beat any odds stacked against me.

This wasn't a list of principles that I had written down and carried around with me. I never even thought about them or realized that I was still living by those same rules as an adult. But when I look back now, I can say with 100 percent certainty that my success both then and now has been thanks to these principles.

The foundation for these rules was laid when I was just a super-determined kid who was trying to turn the impossible into a reality. However, as I grew up and found my dreams and goals expanding, these rules became a recipe that I could follow for certain success. I have put them into practice again and again, in medium after medium. I continue to use them and follow them because they work. They aren't revolutionary on their own, but taken together, they reveal the kind of mindset and work ethic that it takes to reach a dream—any dream.

Over the past five years, we have seen an undeniable shift in the atmosphere for creators of all kinds. Doors are opening. Gates are coming down. Creatives and artists are more valuable than ever, not just for consumers, but also for businesses and brands. Every platform is evolving in a way that welcomes more creators, and a more diverse palette of creators, to the table. We're seeing a higher level of demand than ever before for shocking, stunning, beautiful creations and voices in every medium. There is real reason to be excited and to celebrate the future of art.

However, despite the enormous demand for creatives, no one seems to be talking about this boom in business. Certainly, no one is encouraging artists to keep at it or telling them how to get themselves into one of those new seats at the table.

Many young people are still abandoning their creative dreams for graduate school or a nine-to-five after the slightest rejection on social media. Others go viral one time, and then we never hear from them again. Still others continue to try to grind it out the old-fashioned way. They pay hundreds of thousands of dollars to go to a prestigious school just to pursue their art, only to be beaten down by a system that tells them that their art isn't meaningful or that it should be one way when it is naturally another. These folks never even have a chance to connect with their audience or to figure out who their audience even is. You have no idea how mad this makes me!

But the main reason that more people don't make it as a creative? They simply do not have a plan.

Singing was always *my* dream. However, a lot of artists and other creators are the products of their parents' or someone else's dreams for them. You'll never get to the top of the mountain if you're following someone else's path. You need a plan of your own.

I can always spot the people who are spurred on by their own relentless momentum, because behind all of their hard work and sac-rifice is a generous spirit. When you boil it all down, real artists are motivated by a passion for sharing. Yes, of course we want to be in front of an audience and be celebrated for our work. We want to be noticed or have our work noticed, sure. But we also want to give something away.

Artists are passionate about sharing something unique, different, or beautiful—whether it's a sound you've never heard before, an ap-proach or style that surprises you or makes you laugh, or a way of looking at something that brings you a smile or an overwhelming flood of emotion. The real goal isn't just the art itself or even profiting from that art. It's sharing that art with the world and using it to make an impact.

I wanted to write this book as a way to do just that, to share what I have learned with anyone who needs to hear it. These are the prin-ciples I have lived by on my path to greatness and success. These are the principles that I still live by today.

I guess a book about mastering your chosen artform and finding success should define exactly what success is. This is where it is important to remind you that you are reading a book by Jason Derulo! If you don't already know, you will soon find out that I am proudly and markedly all about the mainstream. Success to me is all about eyeballs, sharing, downloads, and sales.

My definition of success has always been about interaction and impact. To be the "best" is to be the most played and most shared, period. I want the numbers on my side. The more people that like something, the more of an emotional impact you make, the more your work connects with someone on a personal level, the better and the more successful it is. Making your way into someone's emotions gains you a follower for life.

However, connecting with someone on an emotional level through art is both hard and easy. Whatever your personal superpower is—humor, emotion, passion, articulation, or relatability—you will need to use it to drive those numbers and engagement.

I have never defined success by anyone else's standards, so when I reached the type of success that clicked with my own definition, it belonged to no one but me.

So what *isn't* success? To me, success has nothing to do with awards, notoriety, fame, pats on the back, mentions, or advertising deals. You won't impress me with anything but reach, interaction, and numbers. How many people bought it, downloaded it, watched it, and shared it with their friends? How many tickets and records did you sell?

This might sound reductive, but instead I see it as liberating. Guess what? The numbers, downloads, and eyeballs are all available to you *right now*. People are scrolling TikTok looking for something that blows them away or surprises them. They are flicking through Instagram and watching their tenth YouTube video in a row just waiting for something to give them a jolt.

In today's world, you don't need an Oscar nomination or a comedy special or an art degree to reach the people and, therefore, to reach success. Unlike when I was trying to break into this business, you don't even need a record label. All those barriers I talked about earlier? They're gone. Poof. There is literally nothing and no one standing in your way.

Yes, numbers are what I'm after, first and foremost. But listen: they aren't everything. There is another level to success that I want to make sure you understand. A big part of it is how you feel about what you're creating. Other people's opinions aside, did you like what you put out? Did it teach you something, make you feel something, or spark with you? The numbers don't come immediately or consistently, so the other marker of success has to come from inside of you.

You're going to hear about my successes, sure, but the best teaching tools I can offer you are actually my failures. Failures, to me, happen when either one of these hallmarks of success is missing. Either something I created didn't get the numbers I wanted, or I wasn't happy with what I put out there in the end. If I'm being real, though, I've written songs that I loved that didn't hit the way I expected them to, and I consider them to be failures, too. To me (personally), the numbers are and always will be king.

For those of us who are deeply motivated by this kind of artistic pursuit, fame and money are not the end goals. No doubt they are nice to have. I don't have these sponsorship deals and post these advertisements for nothing. Today, I want to make money to show Black kids that they can make money using their brains. But (honestly) those perks aren't why we get into this in the first place.

Let me speak for myself. They aren't why *I* got into this in the first place. Number one, I wanted to be undeniably great at my craft—the best, actually. Number two, I wanted to get to the top of the mountain in terms of my reach. Number three, I wanted to give something away to my audience and to all of the other creatives coming up behind me.

If you start with a primary goal of making money, your success will be short-lived. Leading with passion will always take you further. Life is short, and if you don't love the art you're creating and enjoy the road you're taking toward your goal, what is the point? When your life is coming to an end, do you want to be able to look back and say, *I made a lot of money*, or, *I made the best memories and enjoyed every day*? For me, the destination has nothing on the amount of fun, satisfaction, fulfillment, and joy that I've experienced throughout the process.

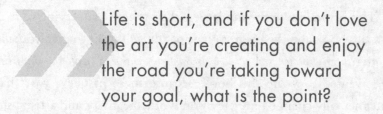

Life is short, and if you don't love the art you're creating and enjoy the road you're taking toward your goal, what is the point?

Really try to get clear on what you want to get out of this artistic pursuit of yours. I bet that deep down, you aren't motivated most of all by fame and money, either. If you are, put this book down, and go find the bookstore's business and investing section! You won't find anything in these pages about shortcuts, cheat codes, manipulating algorithms, or turning a dime into a dollar. You *will*, however, find inspiration, hard-won lessons, fuel for your aspirations, encouragement, and insight into today's new landscape for creators.

No one knows this landscape better than I do. At the time that I'm writing this, I have sold more than 250 million records since I started perfecting those songs back in high school. I am one of only six artists ever to have had a number one song in three separate decades—a nod to how young I was when I started this thing, not to how old I am now, you hear? I have had twelve number one songs, have recorded five studio albums, and have toured internationally in more countries than I can count. I am still performing international sold-out tours today.

But if you ask me what I am most proud of, I will tell you without a doubt that it is the content I have made over the past few years through my collaborations on TikTok. Because it is one thing to be great at a single artistic pursuit like singing, but it is another thing altogether to start something new and find the same level of success with it. This kind of winning on multiple platforms comes down to planning, determination, and execution. It comes down to having a clear set of rules for your art and putting those rules to work.

This brings me to the fundamental argument I am trying to make with this book and the biggest piece of advice I want to give you: *there has never been a better time to be a dreamer, a creative, a creator, or an artist.*

I wanted to write this book because these past few years have fundamentally changed my views on work, creativity, and artistic success. We don't live in the same world today that I came up in. When you upload a song, a story, a comedy sketch, or a piece of artwork today, it can actually help you start down your path to greatness. But that's if—and only if—you're willing to put in the work off-line, too.

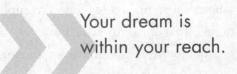

Your dream is within your reach.

Your path and your journey won't look exactly like mine, and they shouldn't. But the principles I am sharing with you here can be applied to any path and any journey. You can take these rules and go crush it on stage, in the classroom, in your office, or wherever it is that you want to be.

Your dream is within your reach. And since I love helping other people achieve their dreams as much as I enjoy chasing my own, I'm going to show you exactly how to grab yours and—even more important—how to hold on to it.

Make no mistake, though. Reading this book will be the easy part. Anyone who knows me will tell you that I've got all the stories. I'm excited to share them with you, along with what I've learned from everything I've been through. But once you put the book down, it's up to you. I'll give you the blueprints, but you've got to pour the concrete.

1

TAKE RISKS.

« »

FAILURE IS GOOD.

Inside a tiny acorn is a mighty oak tree.
Trust the process.

—ELLEN DEGENERES

The year was 2009, and I was about to release my debut single, "Whatcha Say." I was still a kid, only nineteen years old, but I had already been singing and writing my own songs for more than a decade. So, to me, it felt like this moment had been a long time coming.

This was a pivotal time in my career—my chance to make it or break it. If the song flopped, my label would probably lose faith in me, and then it would be very difficult to get anyone in the music industry to give me a second chance—not to mention the listeners themselves.

"Whatcha Say" had to work, end of story. Failure was not an option. And I'm not talking about a mild level of success, either. I was shooting for and expecting to break out as a new star on the rise. I wouldn't be satisfied with anything less.

Besides feeling all of this pressure about finally introducing myself to the world in a major way, the song itself felt really personal to me. Before I wrote "Whatcha Say," my older brother, Joey, somebody I've always been close to, came to me and confessed that he had cheated on his girl, who was the mother of his first child. Of course, he felt horrible about the situation and incredibly remorseful. He wanted to earn her forgiveness and to do something to make things right.

"You've got to beg her to take you back," I told Joey.

I tapped into the remorse that I knew my brother was feeling and wrote the song in his voice, as if I was the one begging my girl to take me back after I'd made a huge mistake. The beat J. R. Rotem and I were working with drew from Imogen Heap's brilliant song "Hide and Seek," which was really cool and experimental. I had never heard anything like it, and that's generally what piques my interest—when something feels new and fresh and I find myself wanting to listen to it over and over again. Those are the signs of something special.

The beat was left field, but it did have a pop sensibility with a big melody. So, it was different while still being grounded in what we expect from a popular song. That's exactly how I like to create. There are established "rules" when it comes to writing pop songs, but if you want people to feel something, you have to add a unique twist. To me, that's the essence of being creative—putting your own spin on a proven formula. I've brought this approach to everything I've done, from my songs to my music videos to my social media posts and even to my business endeavors.

When I put it all together, I knew that "Whatcha Say" would make an amazing debut single. But was it enough? I wasn't satisfied. I wanted to make *absolutely sure* that after just the first few seconds of the song, everyone who was listening would know and remember who I was.

You probably already know where I am going with this . . .

I didn't come up with this idea completely on my own. It's actually a pretty popular device in rap for artists and producers to introduce a "tag" at the top of a song. But as far as I knew, it had never been done before in pop music and certainly never been sung.

I wrestled with the decision like crazy. I knew that this one little thing might get me laughed at or written off as corny. But it could also pay off and make it impossible for listeners to forget me.

I played around with a few different melodies that I could use for my name, and I finally found the one that just clicked. You know it. You're probably singing it in your head right now. Sorry if it gets stuck in there, but that's also kind of the point.

Once I was confident that I had the right melody, I knew that it would cut through the noise, so I sang my name at the beginning of "Whatcha Say" and then again on many of my songs that followed.

For more than a decade now, everywhere I go, people ask me to sing my name for them, or to sing *their* name for them, or if they can sing *my* name for *me*. Yeah, it definitely gets old sometimes, but I have no regrets. Would as many people out there know my name and love my songs if I hadn't included that tag? We'll never know. But I definitely wouldn't take the chance of going back and changing anything.

The lesson here is to take risks. In fact, this is me *begging* you to take risks. Stop being boring. Stop being derivative. Stop being scared. Please.

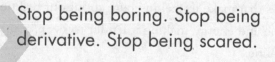

Stop being boring. Stop being derivative. Stop being scared.

I have never seen an artist who was interesting or inspiring who didn't take a massive risk—usually more than one. When someone has put their entire career on the line for one single artistic or creative decision, we can all feel it. There is nothing better. The stakes are high, and therefore, the excitement we feel when we consume that art is high, too. We can immediately sense that we've never heard or seen something like this before.

At first, we're not sure how we feel about it or what we even think. That might sound like a bad thing, but it's the exact position that you want to put people in. You *want* to stun them and then wow them. That's how you'll make them remember you.

That said, some risks fail. Let's be real, *most* risks fail. But don't misunderstand me. I'm not saying to just take any old risk. If you're going to put your art and maybe your whole career on the line, you want to make sure it's for something you stand by and won't regret even if you fall on your face.

This is why my number one rule for taking risks is to make sure that every risk you take is informed by as much feedback, consideration, and prior calculation as possible. This all comes from daily work and an incredible amount of sharing—and actually listening to and incorporating the feedback you get.

This brings me to social media . . .

It is popular these days to hate on social media. We are inundated by the message that social media is harming us, rotting our brains, and ruining our society. Instagram, TikTok, Snapchat, Facebook, and Twitter all encourage us to be divisive, to promote fake versions of our lives that make us feel insecure about our realities, and to deplete our time and energy, making it harder to sleep, connect, and be present off-line.

Okay, now that we have all of that out of the way (and for what it is worth, I agree with all of those statements to a certain degree), I want to tell you why social media is probably the greatest innovation to happen for artists since electricity, and why if you are a creator of any kind who's alive today, you should be bowing down at the feet of social media and giving it your utmost respect, adoration, and attention.

If you want to have a chance of huge success of any kind, you need to make creating content a part of your daily routine. I don't care who you are; there is no way around this. If you are a poet, you need to write poems. Singers, you have to sing. Gardeners, plant seeds. Comedians, you've got to tell jokes. Lawyers, take us to law school with you, teach us about the law. Creators, create. Invite us to the wonderful world of you, whoever that may be.

I know this all seems pretty basic, but it is critical to start at square one. If you aren't either already practicing your craft every day or actively working to make time to practice your craft every day, you have no business reading this book.

There are no shortcuts to success. At least, not my definition of success.

>> If you want to have a chance of long-term success as a creative of any kind, you need to make creating content a part of your daily routine.

You already know that when I was coming up, I was writing songs every day and singing late into the night. There's zero chance that I would have the kind of success I enjoy today if I hadn't done all that. So I will say it again: if you want to have a chance of long-term success as a creative of any kind, you need to make creating content a part of your daily routine. Nonnegotiable. And honestly, that's the easy part.

The tricky thing is figuring out what to do with this content that you're creating every day. Not all of it is going to be great. Maybe you have some experimental poems that you wrote in the shower, a few pages of a novel that you know are just so-so, graphic design that's a bit one-dimensional, or jokes that aren't your funniest. The good news is, you get a gold star for getting after it. This is exactly how you'll get better. The bad news is, the road to mastering your craft will be lined with some stuff that falls a little flat.

If you need some validation here, let me tell you about the origins of the song "Wiggle." When I first wrote that song, the lyrics were, "You know what to do with that big black truck." Yeah, I know. It was terrible. We even recorded the song with those lyrics, and after the session, I was torn. I liked the song, but I was pretty sure it wouldn't go anywhere because of that awful lyric. I didn't fully stand by it, so it wasn't worth it for me to take that risk.

So, yeah. I know a thing or two about the daily grind and the inevitable by-products. It wasn't until we decoded the lyric to, "You know what to do with that big fat butt," that the magic of that song was truly unlocked. We had to fail that first time in order for that magic to ever even become a possibility. But that didn't mean that releasing the song was any less of a risk. It was still a pretty dicey lyric. The only difference was that this time, I believed in it—so I was willing to stake my claim and take that risk.

The truth is, you won't always know what stinks and what doesn't, which risks are worth taking and which ones will land with a giant thud. Sure, you have some idea of what you like and what you don't like, but your opinions are not objective. Until you get feedback from other people, you're mostly running blind.

Oh, did you think that I just trusted my gut on "Wiggle"? Even once I changed the lyric? Hell, no. When I played that second version of the song for people, I paid close attention to how they reacted.

They pretty much all went nuts for it. This response validated what I already thought, but I knew that my opinion wasn't worth all that much without that validation.

So what can you do with the content that doesn't get the best feedback? For the longest time, the answer was . . . nothing. That was the case when I was growing up. All of those songs I was writing during my come-up were essentially meaningless. Yes, they helped me grow. They were a part of the process. That's definitely valuable. But as products themselves, they were worth nothing until I was ready to take a huge leap of faith and try to get signed by a record label.

At that point, I brought what I thought was my best stuff together into a demo and hoped it was good enough to catch people's attention. However, with the dawn of social media, those days are over. For me, it began to change when I started posting songs on Myspace. It was like a calling card. People I met or reached out to could go there and check out my songs.

I was an early adopter of social media as a place to post content, but now, the paths to success in all kinds of industries are blending and blurring and merging with social media in a crazy and exciting way. And that content you may have thought was useless yesterday is perfectly viable to share today. You have a platform with the potential to reach millions upon millions of eyeballs, where you can upload your work for free and receive invaluable feedback. That feedback may come in the form of likes or comments, or it might come in the form of crickets. Either way, pay attention to what your audience is saying, or not saying.

You're already creating daily content. At least, I hope so. Now, start posting it. If you're on the daily grind aspiring toward anything, put it out there. It doesn't matter which platform you choose. All that matters is that you get it out into the universe for people to see, hear, and react to.

People will tell you over and over that you are a brand. Your brand has to have an identity, and therefore, your content has to be consistently this way or that way and always within the confines of your defined brand. That advice is meant to keep you scared, not to mention limited. It is also meant for someone who is already successful, a known entity. That is the time to be diligent about maintaining a brand.

For now, worrying about maintaining a brand identity is putting the cart before the horse, as they say. If the work you're creating is already pretty consistent, great. But as you're growing, this is the best time to experiment and explore. Try something you've never tried before, whether it's in another genre or another voice, or it's something that's just plain wacky. You never know where you might find a spark. It's a lot harder to get away with this once you're more established and people have an expectation of your work.

Your first two jobs as a creator or simply as a pursuer of greatness are (1) to create content and (2) to put it out there. That's it.

If you created something that's a little weird because your creative energy took you in a strange direction today, you might not be sure about whether or not you want to post it to your main account. Why not create a new account under an alias and post it there? Or, if you mainly use TikTok, upload something different to Instagram, or vice versa. Maybe you have thirty-five different accounts, and each of them has a separate point of view. If you're putting in the work and flooding your pages with that content every day, then trust me, you're on the path to success.

This approach works for anyone. The most important thing is to put in the work every day and make it visible to yourself and others. This is how you create accountability for yourself and growth that you can track. As you watch your work change and develop, you'll build a sense of trust in yourself and the confidence you'll need when that risk-taking moment arrives.

Case in point—when I decided to sing my name out loud on "Whatcha Say," it didn't come out of nowhere. I had been writing and recording songs for years and years, and I knew from experience which types of risks had the best chance of yielding big results. This was one of them. And so was "Wiggle," but definitely not with the original lyrics!

As humans, we tend to wait until the moment feels right to do something. *I'll start my diet next week because I'm going out for my friend's birthday this weekend. I'll start putting my art on Instagram when it gets a little bit better. I'll start releasing covers online when I get a videographer. When I have enough money, I'll be able to start my business.* There's always a reason to wait.

Well, fuck that! Start today. Find a way. There's *always* a way. If anything, people will love to watch your journey and will appreciate the realness of the infancy of your art. One day, when you're the beast that you want to become, you'll be so glad you started when you did, and you'll get to look back and see how far you've come.

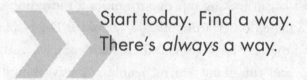

Start today. Find a way.
There's *always* a way.

As you accumulate feedback and learn to trust yourself, you'll start to see opportunities pop up that allow you to take risks and break through. It's important to find a balance between listening to those two things—your own opinions and the feedback you get from others. You'll find that the more you incorporate that feedback and grow as an artist, those two things will become more and more aligned.

Everyone who has succeeded at a high level in any medium has discovered their own magic and done it their own way. There's only one of each of those people, and there's only one Jason Derulo, and there's only one of you. To be honest, that's half of the magic right there.

« »

With all of that being said, it is important to understand that failure is, and will always be, a part of risk-taking. As a creative, innovative person, you're going to fail. It's inevitable, and you've got to know this going in. Don't kid yourself and end up being surprised when it happens.

That said, no one *wants* to fail. So, how do you know when to take a risk and when to try a safer route? The best advice I have for you is to try and minimize the pain of a potential failure by always doing your research, and running toward things that you personally enjoy. If you don't like the risk you're taking, if you don't think it's exceptional in every way, why take the chance? That failure will hurt ten times more and you'll be kicking yourself for gambling on a risk you weren't obsessed with from the beginning.

The best way for me to illustrate this is with investments. A couple of years ago I began seeking out opportunities for investing my savings. I have watched other artists like Jay-Z and P. Diddy build businesses around their art for years, and these businesses, when they work, offer huge and consistent returns. Thinking I was taking the safest possible investment route, and emulating these two legends that I admired, I decided to invest in the "traditional" brands that catered to music artists: clothing and alcohol.

Let me be clear, in hindsight, the investment itself wasn't the mistake, it was the decision to intellectually coast. I didn't do my due diligence, and I assumed that what worked for Jay-Z and P. Diddy would work for me. I didn't stop to think, *Wait, what am I risking here? What do I like about what I am investing in? If this money goes nowhere and disappears, will I be comfortable with the risk that I just took?* The

24

answer—if I had stopped to ask myself these questions—would have been a resounding "no." I had built my entire career on nontraditional choices, so why had I thought investing would be any different? At the end of the day, I lost more than six hundred thousand dollars in these investments in no time at all. Lesson learned.

One of the great gifts of failure, however, is knowledge. A year or so later, I met an entrepreneur and businessman named Danny White. Still sore from my failures, I spent the night grilling him about up-and-coming businesses and cool new ideas that needed financial backing. I could tell he had an idea in mind but wasn't sure if he should bring it up. I told him I was happy to take a risk. The next day, he presented me with graph after graph and spreadsheet after spreadsheet making a compelling and persuasive case for investing in . . . car wash companies. Yes, you read that correctly. I fought with the idea. There was nothing *less* sexy than the neighborhood car wash. But I have to tell you, after doing my research, I was more than convinced. There had been a massive shift and upheaval in the car wash industry, from one-time payments to subscription models. The investment would certainly be a risk, but after spending night after night getting lost in the details, I knew it was one I was willing to take. If the money went "poof," I would still be proud and glad that I went for it. To prove my point about doing research, that car wash company has been one of my greatest financial success stories and stands to make me a boatload of money. Sticking to your own research and following your own rules will lead you down paths you never expected. Danny and I have made so many decisions together that have brought me to new and unforeseen industries, from volleyball to healthcare to fitness. Just one of these investments is valued at more than two billion dollars. I'm so glad I wasn't too scared after my initial investment failures to try something new.

Danny once told me, "Follow your gut. If you are obsessed with the idea, chances are, other people are, too." I remember thinking,

Wait, that's my line! This is advice that I had always followed in the world of music, why wouldn't it work in business as well? The fundamental rules you are reading about in this book are fundamental for a reason—they apply to all success stories in every arena. Once I figured this out, I knew I had to write this book and share this knowledge with you. The moral of the story is this: the majority of the times you take a risk, you'll fall on your face. That's okay. It's actually great, because all you need to do is learn from that failure and get up and do it again. If you fail nine times out of ten, but that tenth time you succeed, that's really all that matters.

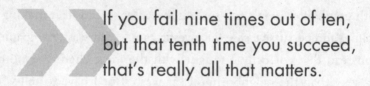

If you fail nine times out of ten, but that tenth time you succeed, that's really all that matters.

Stephen Curry is such an incredible basketball player because he'll miss thirteen threes in a row and then still take that fourteenth shot. Most people don't do that in real life. They fail one time, and then suddenly they're too scared to take another risk. They give up.

Personally, I think this is why a lot of artists retire long before they're out of creative juice. Not me. I'll gladly fail 1,000,000 times, because I know that risk number 1,000,001 is when I'm going to get hot.

Look, nobody likes to fail. It's not fun at the time, but I'm truly grateful for all of the failures that I've had. I'll tell you honestly that every single one of them has been better for my career in the long run than all of my successes combined. I've learned from my failures, I've grown from them, and I've stayed humble because of them. If I could go back in time and turn those failures into successes, I wouldn't do it.

Let me give you an example.

I've made a lot of hits, but not every one of my songs does well, and those things are like my babies. I put my heart into everything I do, but it takes a lot more hours to write and record a song than it does to create a TikTok video. When a song isn't received the way I expect it to be, it hurts.

There's one song in particular that I was really proud of, but that landed with a giant thud: "Cheyenne." When I first heard the bass line to that song, I thought it was really reminiscent of something that Michael Jackson would have done. From the time I was a toddler, Michael has been, and continues to be, one of my biggest inspirations, so I was instantly drawn to the song.

In the writing process, I brought out a lot more of those influences, and my co-writers and I created a story about a long-lost love named "Cheyenne." Once again, it was personal to me, since it was based on a real woman with a different name. As we were writing, I could easily see in my mind what the video would look like: dark and edgy with a lot of imagery of me being trapped and haunted by the memory of Cheyenne. Seeing this imagery in my mind's eye inspired the song even more.

When we recorded the song in the studio, it felt magical. I had even brought in a guitarist named Orianthe, who had played with Michael, to play on "Cheyenne." As soon as she walked into the studio, she told me that she'd been blown away by the record and could feel Michael's spirit in the song.

Hearing that cemented it for me. This was going to be my next number one hit. As I said, there's always a delicate balance between listening to your own opinions and being open to feedback from others. This time around, both things told me that "Cheyenne" was something special, and that this was another pivotal moment that could really change the scope of my career.

It wasn't only Orianthe, either. Everyone I played "Cheyenne" for absolutely loved it. This response made me feel as though I was going to become a different, more respected artist in people's minds once they heard the song.

Yeah, it didn't go down that way.

When we released "Cheyenne," I saw a few glimpses of the kind of success that I expected it to have. Just two weeks after the release, I performed "Want to Want Me" with Taylor Swift as a guest performer on her 1989 World Tour in Washington, DC. After the show, Taylor tweeted about it and mentioned how much she loved my new single, "Cheyenne." This was a huge moment. Taylor's was the highest-grossing tour of that year and was also critically acclaimed. It meant a lot for her to give the song a shout-out.

Later, when I met Michael Jordan for the first time, he told me that "Cheyenne" was his favorite song. That one blew me away. He's one of the most inspirational and influential Black men to ever live, so that was a big deal to me personally.

A lot of critics also mentioned how reminiscent "Cheyenne" was of a classic Michael Jackson song. I assumed that all this love for "Cheyenne" would translate to the masses. Why wouldn't it? But commercially it didn't hit the mark, never mind hitting number one. That song barely scratched the top forty.

While I greatly valued and appreciated the support that "Cheyenne" got from celebrities, you already know that's not how I define success. To me, a song that I expected to hit at number one and that ended up getting little commercial traction is nothing less than a failure. And because this song meant so much to me and I had such high hopes for it, this one really stung.

As I do with all of my failures, I tried my best to put my own disappointment aside and analyze why "Cheyenne" hadn't worked. Where had I gone wrong? "Cheyenne" was definitely one of my darker songs. The video, which was mostly true to my original vision, was dark, too.

I had known that releasing something darker and making a cinematic video for it was a risk. But I felt so strongly that it would pay off that it had seemed more than worth it. This time, I learned that it just wasn't what my particular audience wanted from me. Maybe "Cheyenne" would have done better if it had come from an artist whose songs were known to be a little darker. Despite my disappointment and hurt, this was a valuable lesson.

Over time, failures like this have taught me not to be so precious about my songs. My job is to make art and share it with the world. But once it's out there, I have to let go. It's not easy to do this with something I put my whole heart and soul into. But I can't force my audience to feel the same way about a song that I do. On the other side of creating something meaningful to you, it's more helpful to consider why it succeeded or failed, and move on with this new knowledge in hand.

« »

If you create a product that people don't respond to, all you can do is move on and continue working on your craft. Eventually, you'll get it right, so you might as well enjoy the process in the meantime. One reason I'm not held back by failure is that I'm obsessed with the creative processes of songwriting and video-making.

I loved every minute that I spent writing and recording "Cheyenne." I wouldn't take one of them minutes back. And by the time it was released and then flopped, I was knee-deep in the process of writing and recording more songs—and loving every minute of that, too.

Whatever you're working toward, I'm sure the destination will be cool, but the real magic is in the journey. For me, a driving force has always been not just success, but the path to success. I fell in love with practicing, getting better, and even falling on my face. It's not just me, either. When you think of all the greats—in any field—they're pretty much all in love with the process.

This love is what keeps me from getting too swept away by all of the highs and lows that come with being a creator—because they will come, no doubt. I just keep my head down and focus on what's next and how I can make it as great as it can be. If you keep moving forward and focusing on the work, everything else will come in as it should. You'll start taking risks that absolutely do end up paying off.

This is exactly how it went for me. Case in point: the song "Talk Dirty." Pretty much everything about that song was a risk. First of all, the whole concept for the song was personal in a way that a lot of my other songs aren't. It came from an experience when I was messing around with a girl who wanted me to talk more. She kept asking me, "Why are you so quiet?"

I was so embarrassed. I was like, *Damn, I didn't know that I was supposed to "let it out," so to speak.* I'd been holding everything in.

With time and experience, I realized that I should and could be more vocal in the right moments. I started exercising that muscle, and slowly I got better at it. Eventually, the tables turned, and I became the person who was telling a girl that it was okay to let it out. In other words . . . talk dirty to me.

Then there was the unique sound that we created for the song. On "Talk Dirty," I chose to work with a producer named Ricky Reed, who goes by the name Wallpaper. "Talk Dirty" was one of the first songs he ever produced on a large scale. A lot of artists won't work with a producer unless they already have a bunch of hits under their belt, but Wallpaper had a unique sound. I wanted to go out on a limb and work with someone new who had something fresh and exciting to bring to the table.

All in all, "Talk Dirty" was about as unique as you could get, from the lyrics to the overall sound to the horns that back the hook. There was nothing else like it on the radio at the time. And that's exactly what

I loved about it. Outside of my work ethic, I think that my greatest strength is my willingness to experiment. I love to just try things without any fear, and that's because I'm focused on the process just as much as the outcome.

Before we released "Talk Dirty," I knew that it would either get written off as the trashiest trash or it would be huge. When you do something that far out of the box, you run the risk of being called a genius or being laughed at. To me, either one of those outcomes is better than sticking to the mold and just getting ignored.

Risks fail hard or they succeed big. That's a good thing. Great art is often polarizing. People love it or they hate it. Either way, it makes an impact by forcing them to feel something. That's so much better than having them walk away from your art and just go, "Meh."

Risks fail hard or they succeed big. That's a good thing. Great art is often polarizing. People love it or they hate it.

You can be a trendsetter or play it safe by following trends. Which one do you think is more likely to be ignored? My advice to you is to be disruptive. I never wanted my songs to fit into the mold of what the radio was already playing. While I was writing "Talk Dirty," I was constantly asking myself how I could be polarizing and relatable at the same time. Again, I was putting my own spin on an established formula.

I ended up being laughed at *and* called a genius. The critics were kind of rough on "Talk Dirty," but audiences loved it. "Talk Dirty" hit the top position in several countries around the world and was in the top ten in more than a dozen others, including the US. You already know that my audience and those numbers mean more to me than anything a critic could say.

Meanwhile, Wallpaper has gone on to become one of today's most in-demand producers, and he's come back to work with me on some of my biggest songs, like "Wiggle," "Get Ugly," and "Swalla." I'm so glad I took a risk on him and that I took a risk on that song in general.

Another risk that has paid off for me was to start directing my own music videos. The first time I did, I knew that I was really going out on a limb. I was taking on the full budget for the video and controlling exactly how it was going to be spent. Plus, it was my own success that was on the line, not some other artist's. If the video flopped, I'd be shooting myself in the foot. I needed it to be good.

For that first video, I went all in with the mindset that failure was not an option. That doesn't mean I played it safe. It means that I used every tip I've shared in this chapter to calculate and mitigate that risk as much as humanly possible.

Looking back, this is the same attitude I've used to approach my entire career. In a lot of ways, my whole life has been one huge risk. And while I may be willing to fail on a small scale with an individual song or one TikTok video, I'm absolutely not willing to fail in the big picture. That has never been an option for me.

When I was starting out, people always told me that I needed a backup plan, but I ignored that advice. In my mind, this was what I was doing. It was all or nothing. And that approach has always worked well for me.

Look ahead at the big picture of your career. If you know in your heart of hearts that no matter what, you will not allow yourself to fail in the grand scheme of things, it frees you up to experiment, try new things, take risks, and fail on a smaller scale. Fail badly. It's okay. It's good, actually.

TAKE RISKS.

>> Fail badly. It's okay.
It's good, actually.

Think about it this way: everybody loves a good comeback story. So fail today, and then tomorrow inspire them with the story of how you bounced back. Make them sorry for doubting the person you used to be.

I always tell myself that the person I am today is not the person I am going to be tomorrow. That keeps me reaching for greater and greater heights. I won't lie. When you slip and fall, it can be tough in the moment. It hurts sometimes, for sure. But when you get back up and try again, you're making the future version of you proud of the person you are today. And in the end, that's the only person in this world who truly matters.

2

UNLOCK CLOSED DOORS.

« »

BUT GO THROUGH THE OPEN ONES FIRST.

When I was starting out, there were no doors open to me. I had no connections, no money, and no obvious way to access my dream. But instead of banging my head fruitlessly, I was able to recognize which doors would open more easily than others.

I never would have been able to reach my dream of becoming a singer if I'd kept on knocking at a door that was closed and locked. By swinging open the door that gave way a little bit more easily—songwriting—I was eventually able to get the key to open the door to my real dream.

« »

When I was four years old, I was sitting on the floor in my family's living room in front of our small TV. On the screen was Michael Jackson performing live in Bucharest, Romania, on his Dangerous World Tour. Staring at the TV screen, I was completely mesmerized by every detail of the performance.

"Ma," I said, turning around to look at my mom, who was sitting on the couch behind me folding laundry. Growing up, I don't think I ever saw her just sitting around relaxing. If she wasn't working, she was doing something around the house, making the most out of the little we had. "I'm gonna be like him one day," I told her. "That's what I'm going to do."

My mom just smiled down at me with pure love in her eyes. She would never dissuade me from following my dreams, but even at that age I could tell that she thought it was just a fantasy. Honestly, I didn't care. I knew that I could dominate on a stage like that one day. If Michael could do it, I reasoned, then why couldn't I?

That was the day that I started singing every chance I got. I'm not talking about singing every once in a while the way other kids might, even other kids who really liked to sing. I sang *all the damn time*—every waking moment of every day. I had a decent voice, and the more I sang, the better I got.

My family noticed my obsession with singing. They thought it was cute, and they were happy to give me plenty of opportunities to practice singing in front of a crowd. When I was a kid, my huge family held birthday parties literally every weekend. My mom was the youngest of fifteen siblings, and almost all of those families lived close by. Fifteen! Honestly, I don't even know exactly how many cousins I have. It's probably somewhere in the hundreds.

My mom and her siblings were born in Haiti. When she was a little girl, her brother Tipaul came to the States, and once he could afford to, he sent for each of his siblings, one by one—a classic immigrant story. After everyone had arrived in the US, the whole crew lived in New York for a few years and then migrated down the coast to South Florida.

By the time I was born, my family had taken over an entire neighborhood in Carol City, a town that's about a half an hour north of Miami. I'm not even exaggerating when I say that we took it over. I grew up in a cul-de-sac where every townhouse was occupied by at least one of my aunts or uncles and their families.

On my block alone, there were about twenty of my cousins who were all born within ten years of me. The rest of my relatives lived right around one corner or another. I was closest with my brother, Joey, and my two cousins Harry and Henry. They were six years older than me and were like triplets. That was my crew, and all three of them now work with me. Family was a constant, everyday thing for me growing up, and still is.

Since I was always singing anyway and I was the best singer in the family, it became my job to sing "Happy Birthday" solo in front of the big-ass crowd that gathered for every single party. With all of them people, we celebrated at least one birthday every week, sometimes even more. There's only fifty-two weeks in a year, and my family had a lot more folks in it than that.

Those parties were lit. I don't know how we managed to squeeze a hundred or more people into our houses every weekend. Growing up, we were far from rich. Carol City was known to be a pretty rough area, and my parents and their siblings hustled and sacrificed just so they could afford their tiny houses there. It was nothing like the way I live today. I came out of the trenches, and I make sure to never take that for granted.

At every family party, the greeting process took at least twenty minutes. It didn't matter that we saw each other all the time. Every woman needed a kiss on the cheek, and every man needed a handshake and a hug. It was all love and all food. So. Much. Food. Chicken and rice, plantains, and my personal favorite, griot, a classic Haitian-style fried pork.

My mom and my aunties cooked so much that they actually built up a tolerance to the hot oil. I once joked on TikTok that my mom didn't even need to use cooking utensils because she could just reach into the sizzling oil and flip the meat with her bare hands. Honestly, though, I wasn't kidding. My mom and aunties never really felt the heat. The smells were insane, and the noises were loud and joyful. That was home to me.

Meanwhile, my dad and my uncles were all about Haitian music, Haitian rum, and dancing. I usually chilled with them. My uncle Jacques would give me a dollar to perform MC Hammer dance moves in front of our relatives, and I always sang to the birthday girl, boy, uncle, or auntie.

Those weekly parties are where I cut my teeth as a performer. Let me tell you, that was a lot of practice. All of my relatives who were watching me just thought I was a cute little kid having fun, but I knew deep down and without question that I was preparing for something much bigger.

My obsession with singing only grew from there. I wasn't like a normal kid who hung out with friends or watched TV after school. Instead, I was locked in my room singing along at the top of my lungs to Michael Jackson, Usher, or Tevin Campbell.

My parents wanted to support me the best they could, but this was a whole new thing for them. They were immigrants just trying to get by. There was no one in our family or in our circle in the music or entertainment industry, so they had no idea where to start.

Still, my mom never made me feel like my dreams were out of reach. When she saw how obsessed I was, she signed me up for a performing arts summer camp. I don't even know how she was able to afford that, but I loved it there and was totally in my element. At the end of the summer, she asked to speak to the chorus director.

"I don't know what to do with him," my mom said. "He sings all day. What should I do?" The director encouraged my mom to enroll me in a performing arts school, so that's what she did.

I started attending Bethune Elementary School of the Arts, which was more than an hour and a half away from my house. That's right—I had the same long commute in elementary school as I did in high school. From that young age, I had to wake up at four in the morning to get on the five o'clock bus to school, and round trip I was spending three or four hours on that bus every damn day. I never really minded, though, because going to Bethune gave me the chance to sing even more.

I sang whenever I was at home, and I sang with the chorus at school. And I made sure that my voice was always the loudest in the group, so that everyone could pick me out of the pack. At school, I also started learning music theory and how to read music, which were great skills for me to learn so young.

The funny thing was, with all of this time and practice singing, I started having trouble figuring out *what* to sing, because I could not remember the lyrics to any songs. I had no problem with the melodies, but I was hopeless when it came to the lyrics. My brain has always been kind of funny that way, and it still is. It picks and chooses what it wants to remember, and when it comes to people's names and song lyrics, I don't stand a chance.

It didn't take me long to realize that I had no problem remembering lyrics when I wrote them myself. So I started writing songs. I began freestyling melodies and lyrics, and it turned out that I was really good at it. Plus, it was fun.

Soon, I was fully in the zone of creating my own music. During those long bus rides to and from school and even when I was sitting in class, I was busy thinking up melodies, dreaming up ideas for songs, and writing them down in my notebook. It was so all-consuming that I had trouble concentrating on my schoolwork. At one point, my teachers thought I had ADHD because I was so distracted all the time. But I was just lost in my own world of making music.

There is nothing in the world like sitting down in a room to write a song. It's just me and the four walls. I have no clue what I'm going to create, where my creativity is going to take me, or what the song will end up sounding like. I just ask myself, "What's on your heart today?" and we go from there.

Sometimes the words come when I'm alone; other times the magic happens in a group. For example, when I wrote the song "Swalla," I was collaborating with LunchMoney Lewis, who's a friend of mine from childhood, J Kash, and Wallpaper. I was really into a Jamaican reggae vibe at the time, and I was listening to a bunch of reggae tunes in the car on the way to the studio. They reminded me of my childhood, when my sister was obsessed with Jamaican music. But I'm Haitian, so I thought it would be cool to take a reggae vibe and add a compas feel to it. Compas (or *konpa* in French Creole) is the most popular style of music in Haiti, and it draws from jazz and merengue.

From the car, I called Wallpaper and explained all of this to him. By the time I got to the studio, he had an amazing beat ready and waiting. LunchMoney and J Kash joined us, and the four of us sat around listening to the beat and humming. Then, out of nowhere, LunchMoney sang out, "Shimmy yay, shimmy yay, shimmy yah . . ." The rest of us just burst out laughing. It was this great, joyful moment, and everything from there flowed like butter. The song basically wrote itself.

I sent the song to Nicki Minaj, and she told me, "I'm getting on this shit."

Nicki wrote her verse and sent it back to me, and it was incredible. The same thing happened with Ty Dolla $ign. At that point, I knew we had created an animal. The whole process of writing and putting that song together was just plain fun, as songwriting often is for me.

Back when I was a kid discovering my love of songwriting, it never changed my goal to become a singer. If anything, my songwriting strengthened my desire to sing, because I knew that I wouldn't have any trouble remembering my lyrics if I wrote them myself. Plus, the songs I wrote were assets that helped me stand out from the crowd.

In Miami, everyone is trying to get it. Wanna-be singers are like crabs in a bucket. By the time I was a young teen, I was anxious to start my career, but I was a total unknown. I was well aware of all the obstacles stacked against me, and from the outside looking in, it seemed that I was facing a losing battle.

I didn't let that stop me, though, and I didn't waste my time dwelling on the obstacles, either. Whenever I've hit a dead end throughout my career, I've always taken this approach: *Okay, that didn't work. What are we going to try next?*

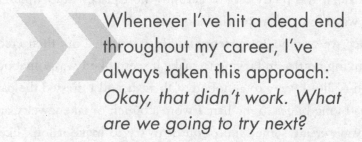

>> Whenever I've hit a dead end throughout my career, I've always taken this approach: *Okay, that didn't work. What are we going to try next?*

I knew that the producers I wanted to work with as a singer were trying to get their songs placed with big artists. So I devised a plan to help them by becoming a part of that journey. If they didn't want to work with me as an artist, then maybe I could convince them to work with me as a songwriter. Then I could use that as a springboard to something bigger.

First, I needed a demo. I was able to buy some inexpensive recording equipment, and Joey, Harry, Henry, and I worked together to figure out how to use it. Let me tell you, it was a lot of trial and error. Those guys have been my core team since way back then.

We started off recording in my house, but we were too loud. It was keeping my mom up, and she had to get up early in the morning to go to work. She's always supported my dream, but she wasn't willing to give up her sleep for it. So we moved the equipment to Harry's house, and that became my de facto studio. Over the course of months, we recorded a bunch of songs, and then we picked a few that we thought were the best and burned them onto a CD.

That was the easy part. Now the question was how to get that demo into the right hands. We had the idea to try to build up some local buzz before trying to get in with producers. So our first stop was the clubs. Every weekend, the four of us went to all the hottest clubs in Miami. The other guys were in their early twenties, but I was nowhere near twenty-one. As long as it wasn't the Hard Rock in Fort Lauderdale, it was pretty easy to get into most places. Sometimes, all it took was a few dollars for the doorman.

Once we were in, Joey, Henry, and Harry maxed out their credit cards buying bottles and trying to make it seem like I was somebody, when in reality I was a total nobody. Oh yeah, and I dressed the part, too. I had long braids in my hair, I wore a bunch of fake jewelry, and we'd always create some kind of outfit to try to make it look like I had fashion sense and money. I had neither. In my white T-shirt, gray vest, jeans, and high-tops, I hoped to stand out.

Then we'd approach the DJ and ask them to play my songs. Sometimes I had to give them a couple dollars or buy them a drink. Most of the time, that did the trick, and they'd put on one of my songs. If not, I'd sit there and bug them—"Come on, man, support hometown"—until they gave in and played it.

The easiest clubs to get into, which were also the most willing to play my songs, were the strip clubs. I grew up pretty fast being exposed to so much at such a young age. When we were in those clubs, I felt so uncomfortable. I had no idea how to act. I wanted people to think I was a star, not some awkward kid. I was looking at everyone else to try to figure out how I was supposed to act. I've learned a lot in my life by just watching other people.

Whether it was at a strip club or a regular dance club, whenever the DJ played one of my songs, I paid close attention to how the crowd responded. Most of the time, the club didn't skip a beat. It didn't create some huge moment, but it wasn't a big record screech, either. It just fit in naturally with the music the DJ was already playing. That was exactly what I wanted, to keep the party going. Seeing everyone continuing to dance and have fun to my music was incredibly validating.

Along the way, I got to know every DJ in Miami. One of them was also the program director at a radio station. He wanted to sign me to a record deal that would give him 75 percent of all the money I'd earn *for the rest of my career.* For life, people! I may have been young, but I wasn't stupid. There was no way I was going to sign something like that. Of course, I felt like he might have been blackballing my songs from the station—even once I was a bona fide star.

The crazy thing was, a lot of other artists in Miami were actually taking this deal. Then he would play their songs on his radio station and at the clubs where he DJ'd, and this helped their careers take off.

There was one artist in particular, who was about my age and came from the same area I did. He signed with this DJ, then got a bigger deal, and was performing all over Miami. Watching him becoming a local phenomenon gave me pause. I felt as if I was looking at a version of who I could've been. Had I made the right choice?

Looking back, I'm so glad that I stuck to my guns. I don't know where that artist is now, but I wish him the best. Meanwhile, this DJ ended up with a terrible reputation around town thanks to all the shiesty stuff he was doing with those artists.

At the same time, I started approaching producers with my first demo. I'd tell them I was a songwriter and go in and play my songs for them. I also put all of my songs on Myspace, hoping to get some attention the grassroots way.

It was a nonstop hustle. I was singing and writing songs constantly, posting them on Myspace, sending them out to producers, and hitting up the clubs. Oh yeah, and I had just started high school! When one door closed, I just kept moving and looking for the next one to tear open.

Though no one was buying my songs—yet—I was meeting and connecting with a lot of producers, and those were valuable connections. One team, the Fliptones, liked my songs and let me record at the studio they used, Studio Center. This was the first large-scale studio I'd ever worked in, and it was an amazing facility. Previously, I'd only recorded in the makeshift studio that we'd created in Harry's basement.

I was excited to finally be able to create a polished, professional-sounding demo, but the first time I went into the studio to record, I had two opposite reactions at once. I was blown away by the million-dollar facility. But I was also shocked to see that the place was a wreck, and there were guns scattered everywhere. I was no stranger to rough environments, but I'd never experienced anything like that in the world of music.

It turned out that Studio Center was owned by the Zoe Pound, one of the biggest and most ruthless Haitian gangs around. The Fliptones just used the studio to record. My time at that studio was a mix of learning how to work with professional equipment and interacting with heavy hitters from the Zoe Pound. As always, I tried to keep my head down and focus on the work. I was appreciative of the time they gave me in that space.

Finally, after what felt like a lifetime of grinding, I got a small break. A DJ I had met named Nu Jerzey Devil had a connection to the rapper Pitbull and played him a song of mine called "Hush." Pitbull agreed to be featured on the track just for the love of it.

I posted the song on YouTube, and Joey, Henry, Harry, and I traveled all over Florida trying to get it into the hands of DJs at clubs and radio stations. But we didn't have a lot of money to put behind it. Even grassroots efforts require dollars to really gain traction.

Nothing much came of that song, but the credit did give me a shred of credibility. This led to some doors starting to open a little bit faster and a little bit wider. I was sixteen when I placed the song "Bossy" with Birdman. But the pivotal moment came when P. Diddy brought the TV show *Making the Band* to Miami.

It was 2005. I was finishing up high school, and the newest iteration of *Making the Band* featured Diddy trying to put together the next hot girl group. As with every season of the show, they needed original songs for the bands to sing. This time, it was all happening in Miami.

Diddy had hired the producer 7 Aurelius to find songs for the show. 7 had worked with a lot of big artists like Ashanti and Ja Rule and was looking for new songwriters in Miami. Thanks to my years of relentlessly hounding every DJ and producer in the city, one of them mentioned my name to 7.

When I walked into the studio to meet with 7, I saw handwritten signs all over the room that said things like "#1 in multiple countries!" and "Biggest artist in the world!" He was for sure trying to manifest something. There was a fog machine pumping out steam and a screen on the wall playing Prince's "Purple Rain" on repeat. In the corner were two doves, who 7 told me were named Peace and Love. He was a character.

Without any more chitchat, 7 played me a beat and said, "Okay, you've got ten minutes to write something." He put the CD with the beat in a boom box and left the room.

I listened to the beat a few times and scrambled to write something before 7 came back in the room exactly ten minutes later. The song was called "In My House," and it was a women's empowerment anthem that I knew would be along the lines of what Diddy wanted for the show. 7 listened. "This is great," he said. "I could really use you."

The next thing I knew, 7 introduced me to Diddy, and I spent the next couple of months writing songs for *Making the Band*. It was an exciting time, but the deals I was making were terrible, and I didn't really make any money from those songs.

This is how it is in the music industry. Producers get paid for their work whether a song is successful or not, but that's not the case for songwriters. They only get royalties when a song hits big. It's still this way today, and I think it should change.

Still, I felt like all of my hard work was paying off in the form of positive momentum. Each new connection I made brought me closer to recording a song of my own. Just as I was about to graduate from high school, I felt that my time was finally coming. There was only one problem: my mom, who insisted that I go to college instead of pursuing my career full-time.

I fought her tooth and nail, but at the end of the day, I respected my mom's opinion too much to go against her. We've always been real close, and I knew how hard she and my dad had worked for me to be able to go to college at all. She had saved up some money for my tuition. Between that, a scholarship, and a substantial loan, we were still barely able to cover the expense.

After a lot of arguing, my mom and I finally came to a compromise. "Give me two years," she told me, and I agreed.

I spent exactly two years—no more, no less—at the American

Musical and Dramatic Academy (AMDA) in New York City. The curriculum there was really tough, and it stretched me for sure. I was learning all kinds of things I'd never touched before: ballet, tap, and even Shakespeare. I threw myself into it and tried to learn as much as I could, even though I really wanted to be in the studio singing my own songs. I knew that I was lucky to be there at all, and I was determined to make the most of it.

Some days were easier than others. One night, I spent five hours rehearsing a Shakespearean monologue that I had to perform in class the next day. But when it was my turn to perform, I suddenly blanked on everything I had learned. It was as if my brain had just pressed delete on the monologue that I had worked so hard on.

The teacher, Professor Pearson, was known to be mean as hell. Rumor has it that he's scared some students so badly that they peed their pants in class. For real. And he ripped into me right away, too. "You will never amount to anything because you don't care about this, and you don't put in the work," he told me. "Why are you even here?"

I have to tell you—this broke me a little bit. But I don't blame Professor Pearson at all. I would've said the same thing if I was the one teaching that class. He had no way of knowing how much I did care or how hard I had actually worked on that monologue. But instead of peeing my pants that day (thank goodness), I resolved to work even harder.

New York is obviously all about theater, and while I was there I caught the bug a little bit. I started to think that was going to be my path. I was still writing songs and doing my schoolwork, and I started auditioning for Broadway shows on top of it.

After many, *many* auditions, I landed the role of Benny in the national tour of the musical *Rent*.

I was hyped. Instead of jumping at the role, though, I forced myself to slow down and really think about it. Of course, it was tempting to say yes. It was a great role and a great show, and most important, it was a job—one that paid!

I still hadn't made one dollar from my music, and I was seriously broke. Some days, I was living off four bananas because they were only twenty-five cents each. I could survive on one dollar a day, and this helped me stretch my money through the month. (No one told me that eating that many bananas would make me constipated. I had to learn that one the hard way.) So the idea of getting a steady paycheck for performing sounded pretty good.

On the other hand, theater wasn't my dream. For many people, including a lot of my classmates, it was the be-all and end-all, and I respect that, but it wasn't that way for me. My goal had always been to become a recording artist, and that hadn't changed. So why take this side step now?

Sure, plenty of stage actors have gone on to record music, but they're still known primarily as theater artists. I worried that if I took the show, I would end up getting locked into theater, and my dream of being a recording artist would be lost. So I turned down the role, and I stopped auditioning. I figured that if I wasn't going to take the gigs when I got them, there was no point in auditioning to begin with.

This is one of those moments that I look back on and wonder whether I'd have the career I do now if I had made a different decision. At the time, it felt good to be able to put all of the hours and energy that I'd been using preparing for and going on auditions back into songwriting. While I was at AMDA, I was able to place a few more songs with different artists, including a song for Lil Wayne, "Coming Home" for Pixie Lott's multiplatinum debut album, and "Test Drive" for Japanese singer Jin Akanishi. No, I didn't sleep much, but I was enjoying every minute that I was awake.

When an artist recorded one of my songs, I went into the studio with them as their vocal producer. It was amazing to be in the room with these artists, and I was grateful for these opportunities. But a small part of me was always wishing that I was the one doing the singing. (Not *that* small of a part, if I'm being real.) No disrespect to those artists, but I had written those songs, and I always knew deep down that they would have sounded better if I was the one who was singing them, too.

Toward the end of my two years at AMDA, I got a message on Myspace from a producer named J. R. Rotem, who had started his own record label, Beluga Heights, as part of Warner Brothers Music. Beluga Heights had signed a new artist named Sean Kingston, and the label was making a name for itself within the industry. J. R. liked the songs of mine he'd heard so far, and he started sending me beats to see if I could write some songs for Sean.

The timing ended up being perfect. I had stayed true to my word and completed my two years of college, just as I'd promised my mom. And although I'd learned a ton while I was there, I had no plans to continue. Up to that point, I had always had to balance working on music with my schoolwork. Finally, I could go full-throttle working exclusively on my craft and my career.

« »

It was 3:00 a.m., and I was back in Harry's basement with Xavier, a friend of mine from middle school. We'd already been working for six hours. J. R. had been sending me beats every week to write songs with. That night, we'd already written one song called "Teacher." I thought it was pretty good and that we'd exhausted all the good beats. Plus, I was exhausted myself, but Xavier wanted to keep going.

"Come on, man, let's write another song," he said. Xavier was writing with me, but he wasn't really a writer. He was mostly acting as a sort of coach, prodding me to come up with stuff and cheering me on.

"Naw, man," I told him. "There's no more dope beats in here."

Finally, I agreed to go through the beats one more time, and I picked the one I hated the least. "Teacher" was a little bit slower, so this time I found one that was upbeat and catchy. I started playing around with it, contemplating how I could draw from my own life to create a lyric around the beat.

I thought about how most up-tempo beats like that were about trying to find love or falling in love. They were never about break-ups. But what if I wrote a breakup song that was really positive and uplifting?

Back in high school, I had dated a girl who was in college. So she was a little bit older than me. After we had been dating for a while, I saw her out with another guy. I was so upset and, of course, angry, too. I had really cared about her.

When I called her on it, I expected an apology or at least some sort of explanation. Instead, she said, "You shouldn't question me. You need to focus on yourself and get your shit together."

Damn. I was devastated, and honestly, it affected me for a long time. I'm not sure if I was ever the same after that. I did start focusing on myself, but at times I probably took it too far. If someone could do that to me, I asked myself, then why give myself to them at all? After that, I was a playboy for a long time, and that experience with my ex brought it on for sure. Being burned so badly at such a young age had led me to lose faith in relationships.

Of course, a lot of good things had also come out of being so hyper-focused on myself. Working so much, there's no way I could have also maintained a relationship. And if I had prioritized a relationship instead, maybe it would have distracted me from my path. We'll never know for sure, will we? But at that moment, I wanted to focus on the positives while drawing from my heartbreak. So I wrote a song about how happy I was to be single and to be celebrating myself and celebrating life.

I'll give you one guess what song it was.

As we wrote, I was surprised by how much I was loving how the song came together. Until then, I never wrote songs when I was tired. But that night, I ended up writing an awesome song. That taught me that magic can still happen, no matter how tired I am. Since then, if anyone I'm working with says, "Let's keep going," I'll never say no.

I wrote "Riding Solo" and "Whatcha Say" before I even had a deal with Beluga Heights. They ended up being two of my first singles, but that wasn't the plan at the time. I was still meant to be writing songs for Sean Kingston, but those songs helped seal the deal.

At that point, Beluga Heights offered me a publishing deal, which meant they would pay me to write songs for their other artists, mostly for Sean. It wasn't a lot of money, but it was the first time *ever* that I was actually getting paid for my work. Plus, I'd be collaborating with J. R. and other great songwriters and spending time in the studio with amazing artists like Sean. It almost seemed too good to be true.

Before the deal was signed on the dotted line, I had to fly to LA to meet J. R. in person. We went into the studio to work together and see if we jelled. By then, I was feeling confident in my abilities, and this time, it was a confidence I had earned. I had been working long enough and gotten enough positive feedback from people I respected to know that I had what it took to succeed. Plus, I knew that I would *do* whatever it took to succeed. That's a powerful combination.

I walked in the first day feeling hyped about working in what I assumed would be a state-of-the-art studio. And that's exactly what I found. I marveled at the controllers, the sound diffusers, and the acoustic panels. It was more than a small step up from Harry's basement, and I could not wait to hear the kind of sounds we could create in there.

Soon, J. R. came in, and after we chatted for a minute, he pointed me toward a door in the corner of the massive studio. Inside was his own studio, which was literally the size of a closet. I had to laugh. I thought I had finally made it big-time, but I was recording in a place that was the opposite of big. I wasn't complaining, though. It still had amazing equipment and was a far cry from Harry's basement, but we were in some close quarters.

J. R. and I spent the entire day together in that studio with him making the beats and me writing the songs. Look, sometimes the magic is there, and sometimes it isn't. You can't force it, and you can't fake it, but we could tell right away that we had it. The chemistry was off the charts, and by the end of the day, we had written seven songs.

As we were working together, I was singing everything we wrote, so J. R. was seeing a whole different side of me. Before that, he thought I was "just" a songwriter. Plus, he was getting to know my work ethic and my personality for the first time. At the end of the day, J. R. turned to me and said, "You should be a recording artist."

I was like, "Yeah, *no shit!*" LOL. Soon after that, I signed a publishing deal with Beluga Heights and a recording deal as an artist in my own right.

This was when things really started to fall into place. I moved to LA and got right to work writing songs, collaborating with Sean, and working on my first album. It felt unbelievable, and I was ready to put in the necessary work to take this thing as far as it could go. I started working harder than ever, spending basically all day in the studio writing song after song after song. Hundreds of them!

For one song that I was writing for Sean, Beluga Heights brought in a talented songwriting duo for me to collaborate with. They were two brothers who went by the name Rock City. We had the beat first, and then we laid down the melody and paired it with a lyric about a guy who can't stop thinking about a girl—as though she's stuck on "Replay." This time, it wasn't based on any one particular story, but we thought the idea behind it was really relatable.

The brothers behind Rock City are from the Virgin Islands. We clicked right away and were able to add a nice island sound to the song. There was no ego in the room that day. We were all just in our flow working together.

Beluga Heights gave Sean the first shot at all of the songs I was writing. He was their biggest artist, and I was still this no-name guy. When the CEO of Warner Music heard some of my songs, he told me, "I try not to say things like this, but 'Whatcha Say' is a number one song." It made sense, then, that the first two songs of mine that they brought to Sean were "Whatcha Say" and "Replay."

I was shocked when Sean and his team passed on both songs. This might have dampened my confidence if J. R. and I, plus the CEO, hadn't believed wholeheartedly in those songs.

J. R. had just signed another young artist from the islands named Iyaz and gave "Replay" to him as his first single. It quickly became a number one hit. Meanwhile, I was able to keep "Whatcha Say" as my first single, and that one became a number one hit, too.

« »

Whenever people ask me for advice about how to "make it," I always think back on this stretch of time in my life. Turning down predatory deals in Miami. Turning down that role of Benny in *Rent*. Taking some other deals that didn't always pay off. Writing songs for other artists when I desperately wanted to be the one performing them. And then taking a publishing deal when I really wanted a recording deal, which very much *did* pay off.

None of these decisions would have been possible without a healthy amount of self-respect and an understanding of my worth. I didn't always have self-worth. I remember when I was a kid, the house I grew up in had two bedrooms. My sister, Kim, begged my parents to help her convert the storage room that was connected to the living room into her own private bedroom. Now it was just my brother and me in our own room. The night she moved out of our room, my brother and I stayed up late talking, and I realized I had been feeling really down. I decided to have a heart-to-heart with him. I felt really insecure and wanted to talk man-to-man (I was nine at the time). "Everything is wrong with me," I told him. "I'm fat, I have acne, I can barely play sports because I have asthma. I'm allergic to everything.

"Why me?" I cried to him, becoming upset.

"You're overreacting. It's not that bad," my brother said. But of course it was to me.

That night, in an effort to cheer each other up, my brother and I started making goals, and later my sister joined in, too. We would put the plastic wrap from the dry cleaners around our clothes at night and go for runs in the neighborhood. I started eating salads for lunch at school.

My dad, realizing what we were trying to do, encouraged us to start lifting weights and showed us how. During commercial breaks, he would tell us to get our reps in.

The first difference was a shift in my mind. With each small change, I grew some confidence. I could do things that were hard, that I didn't think I could do, and that made me more aware of my value as a man. If I could take this one small step, I could take a hundred. I could do anything.

You have to conquer self-worth before deciding your path. You'll never be greater than the person you think you can be. You'll never make more money than you believe you're worthy of. You won't break any records that you don't think you're able to.

Same way that you won't be in a relationship that isn't worthy of you. Or you won't eat bad foods that aren't worthy of your body.

To change your quality of life, you first have to increase your level of self-worth. How much do you value yourself? Whatever your answer is, it's not enough.

UNLOCK CLOSED DOORS.

Have you tried removing the people or things in your life that keep you feeling small? It can be the most painful thing, to be honest with yourself about the things that are actually weighing you down. The people who make you feel like you're not as great as your potential. When you start to remove the damaging components, you'll start to love yourself more, believe in yourself more.

When you've increased the value of the vision you have of yourself, you won't settle for less. You will find: The best group of friends who are likeminded and driven. The best diet to fuel a champion. The best workout regimen to sustain a healthy mind, body, and spirit. The best work routine to achieve your goals at the highest levels. All this because you think the world of yourself and now understand what you deserve.

The lesson here is this—if you want to succeed, there is no doubt you will have to knock down some doors that are standing in the way of your goals. But they'll fall much faster once you are already in the building. So, start with the ones that crack open more easily. Don't be tempted by the ones that swing open but that you know in your gut are leading to the wrong place. And never, ever stop knocking at the ones that have your dreams waiting on the other side.

3

YOU ARE ONLY AS GOOD AS YOUR ROUTINE.

« »

TRAIN REPETITIVELY
FOR YOUR SUCCESS.

Let curiosity, kindness, and grit steer your life and you
will always end up somewhere incredibly interesting.

**—DREW TAGGART AND ALEX PALL,
THE CHAINSMOKERS**

Maybe you picked up this book because you were interested in learning more about me. Well, I hope I've delivered on that. But more likely, you're reading this because you want to be rich, famous, and successful, or at least one or two of those three things. Well, join the crowd. There are tons of folks out there who have the exact same goals and aspirations that you do. Some of them will make it, but the hard truth is that most of them won't.

So, what is the one thing that might actually make the biggest difference between a normal life and an amazing life that you can control? You may be surprised to hear this, but I believe it's a good routine, plain and simple. Success is not a sprint. It's a marathon, and you've got to train for it as though you're preparing to run for the rest of your life.

Most people don't see their work or their art this way, and that's especially true for people who are trying to succeed on social media. They focus on the short term—on one video or one post and how they can make it go viral. You already know that I don't care about *going* viral. Hell, my dog has gone viral—more than once. I'm writing this book because I want to help you *stay* viral. And that requires a routine and a stick-to-itiveness that most people, if I'm being real, simply don't have.

I'll keep saying it, because it's worth repeating: you've got to put in the work if you want to succeed. There's no way around it, so don't bother trying to find one. And, more important, you've got to *keep* putting in the work. It's your job to work yourself into a rhythm of success, and that takes time and a whole lot of effort.

The grind is like medicine to the soul. It keeps you young and hungry. The moment you stop, the moment you lose purpose, your mind, body, and spirit go into starvation mode. The healthiest version of you is the version that is chasing the best version of you. Spoiler alert . . . IT IS IN THE CHASE that you find true happiness. You won't realize this is true until you get to the destination.

I'll keep saying it, because it's worth repeating: you've got to put in the work if you want to succeed.

In my life and throughout my career, there have been certain moments when I was more focused on sticking to my routine than others, and that's consistently when I have had the greatest creative output and found the most success.

A good example is when I first moved to Los Angeles. I was nineteen years old, fresh out of my two-year stint in college, and had just gotten my publishing deal with Beluga Heights. I didn't have a deal with them as an artist yet, just as a songwriter for other artists.

My entire publishing deal with Beluga Heights was for forty grand. I definitely wasn't getting rich off of songwriting, but I didn't care. I was so hyped to be taking concrete steps toward my dreams, and I was determined to utilize that publishing deal as a springboard to eventually launch my career as a solo artist.

When I got to LA, I bought a new car and rented a condo that was well beyond my means. As soon as my mom found out, she flipped. "What are you doing?" she asked me. "You can't afford this!"

"Exactly," I told her. "I got this place *because* I can't afford it."

My mom thought I'd lost my damn mind, and maybe I had, but there was a method to my madness. I knew that living outside of my means would force me to find a way to make money and grab the success that I wanted so badly. My state of mind was all or nothing. I intentionally backed myself into a corner so that I *had* to succeed by any means necessary. There's something to be said for that. Either I'd make it as an artist or I'd get kicked out of my apartment. The stakes were pretty high.

I don't necessarily recommend that other people do this, so don't go calling me if you max out your credit cards with no way to pay them off. It's not for everyone, but it worked for me. And the reason it worked so well is that I built a routine to win.

During those first six months in LA, my schedule did not vary from day to day one little bit. I woke up late every day at around 1:00 p.m.

(you'll see why in a minute), and went directly to the gym without eating any breakfast. Then, I went back to my condo, took a shower, went straight to the studio, and started writing songs. I listened to the songs that I wrote the day before and asked myself, did they have potential? Should I continue working on them? Or did I need to find new magic in another idea? I wrote so much that I became less precious about each song. Each failed idea was an opportunity to start over and create something new. No problem for me because I was obsessed with the grind. If I didn't make a hit yesterday, I get a new chance at it today. I believe that. The irony is, the hit hardly ever comes. I write hundreds of songs before finding the magical one. This goes for everything in life. If we are celebrated for every single thing, the standout moments lose all of their value. We can appreciate our wins more when they are hard to come by.

I worked in that closet-size studio until 3:00 or 4:00 a.m. every single day. Three times a week, I took a dance class. And that was it, literally. I had zero friends in LA, and I didn't know any girls there. My cousin Henry had moved out to LA with me and was working as my recording engineer. It was just me and Henry, grinding it out in the studio. We weren't having a whole lot of fun, at least not outside of the joy we found in creating music, but we were definitely productive.

The best thing about my life at the time was that every day they baked fresh cookies at Chalice Studios, where we worked, and they gave us one free meal. It might sound like I'm playing, but I promise you I am 100 percent serious. Coming right off of being so broke in college, it felt like the biggest deal to me that I could ask for cookies any time. Plus, they had this big binder that was the size of two phone books filled with menus from nearby restaurants. We could order one meal a day.

Most days, that was the only meal I'd eat, so we had to make it stretch. Sometimes, Henry and I ordered something cheap just so we could get a lot of it. Despite the fact that I was rationing my food and living off one free meal and cookies, when I was ordering from that menu book, I felt like I'd made it. I'd finally arrived.

During those six months, I wrote a whole bunch of hit songs, including two number one hits. That time period ended up being pivotal for me. It laid the entire foundation for my career. I credit a lot of my eventual success to the strict routine I kept during that time.

Okay, so you get that building a routine is important. Now you may be wondering *how* to build that routine and stick to it, which is usually the hardest (and most important) part. To this day, no matter what I want to achieve, I create my daily routine by looking at the end goal and working backward, creating a trajectory that's made up of smaller goals that I can complete each day. In other words, I figure out where I'm trying to go and then plot out the steps I need to take every day in order to get there. Then these daily goals become a non-negotiable part of my routine.

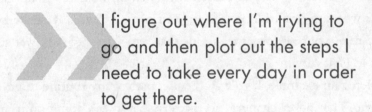

I figure out where I'm trying to go and then plot out the steps I need to take every day in order to get there.

I'm not necessarily a rule follower. I've been coloring outside the lines my entire life. But I always follow the rules that I set for myself. It's a whole lot easier to just follow a rule that you've already set than it is to reinvent the wheel a million times as you stumble toward your goal.

Think of your daily routine as the rules for your life, and then just . . . follow them. That's it. Sometimes the most effective things really are the simplest.

This plan of attack is also helpful because, depending on what you're going after, the end goal may seem unattainable. Sometimes, even I look at my goals and think, *I've never done this before; will I be able to do it?* It's way too easy to go down that rabbit hole, but that don't help nobody. It's a whole lot less intimidating to focus on taking it day by day. If I wake up knowing exactly what I'm supposed to do that day, there's no room for questions or second-guessing or doubt.

There's a famous quote, "If you want something you've never had, you must be willing to do something you've never done before." My version of that is this: "To become someone you've never been, you have to do things you've never done." Challenge yourself to win the day. Get used to winning. This will train your mind to crave that feeling. On the days you slip up, there's no need to beat yourself up about it. It happens. Go twice as hard the next day.

This doesn't mean that your daily goal or routine is going to be easy. Mine almost never is. That daily routine might be its own challenge, but it's still going to be less intimidating than the main goal you're working toward. If you keep your eye on that daily challenge, you can let yourself forget all about that big, scary goal and yet still reach it. That's a win.

Here's an example. It's always been a part of my routine to go to the gym. That never changes, no matter what else is going on in my life. But there are times when I'm trying to stay in shape, and there are other times when I'm trying to get in *crazy* shape.

When I'm trying to get my body to an amazing place, I set a goal to work out three times a day—lifting twice and getting some cardio in once. No lie, that's not easy, physically or mentally. But it's still way less daunting than the bigger goal of completely transforming my body. As soon as I set that daily routine, I stop thinking about the bigger goal, and all I have to worry about is getting through each daily challenge, one workout at a time.

Setting up your routine before you have to execute it also primes you so that when the time comes, you're mentally ready. If your goal is to post more or gain more of a following on social media, plan out your content in the morning before you go to work or school. Then you know exactly what you need to do later that day. All you have to do is film it and post it.

My advice is to post at least once every single day. This will help you get used to that rhythm and teach you really quick what works and what doesn't so you can keep improving as you go.

Beyond all of these practical reasons, for me, committing to a routine is the ultimate motivator. Once I promise myself that I'm going to do something, I don't want to call myself a liar. There are always so many excuses to not follow through on any goal, whether it's to get to the gym or to put in whatever work you need to do in order to succeed. Nine times out of ten, if you take the easy road you'll feel like crap afterward. But if you follow through on your plans, you'll never regret it. Every time you achieve your daily goal, you are giving yourself a chance to feel yourself winning. This programs your mind so it gets used to that feeling and you develop an expectation of winning.

If you find that you're lying to yourself and taking advantage of those endless excuses more often than not, you may want to look deeper to figure out why. Do you really want this shit or not? If not, then you need to reassess your larger goal and figure out what you really do want.

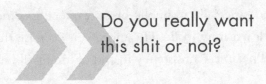

Do you really want
this shit or not?

If you do truly want it but you aren't taking the necessary steps, this usually comes down to a fear—fear of failure or fear of putting yourself out there. We've already tackled failure. But putting yourself out there is a battle for almost everyone.

A lot of us are our own worst enemies. No matter how confident we seem on the outside, deep down we care too much about what other people think. If you're not careful, this can easily keep you from reaching your goals.

If I'm being real, I feel this way sometimes, too. The number one hardest thing for me to do is to figure out how to put myself out there authentically on social media and still be compelling. This is a talent, and like any talent, it takes a lot of time and practice to develop.

But let's back up for a quick second. What does it even mean to be your "authentic self"? None of us is one-sided. We're different when we're telling a joke from how we are when we're sad or angry or when we're around certain people. It's impossible to get all sides of yourself into one video or social media post. So how can you reveal those different levels that added together make you unique?

To back up even further, the truth is that a lot of us don't know who our full "self" even is. We don't speak enough to have developed an authentic voice, so how are we supposed to share that voice with the world? Seriously, think about how often you speak to people, and I mean *really* speak. You probably do it a lot less than you think.

Most of us are lacking conversation in our lives. I'm for sure not the most talkative person myself, but there are plenty of people out there who talk way less than I do. This, too, comes with practice. Speaking in general, and especially in public or on camera, is something that you have to learn how to do. The more you exercise that muscle, the better you'll be at it. Consistency in and of itself will help you find your voice.

It's still possible to doubt yourself, though, even if you're great.

I've been putting out songs since I was fifteen years old, and I still feel a little bit self-conscious when I release a new one. No matter how amazing I think a song is, I never know for sure how other people will react until it's out there. What if they hate it?

The best way I've found to get past this self-doubt is to force myself to stick to the plan. This is why it's so damn important to have a plan to begin with! Line everything up—exactly what you're going to do each day, when you're going to do it, and so on. Once you've written it all down, you've made a decision about what you're going to do. It's done. There's no reason to waste time and energy second-guessing or deciding all over again just because you started doubting yourself. The stronger you wrote that down for a reason. Have trust in that person, and tackle what's next on that preset agenda.

> The best way I've found to get past this self-doubt is to force myself to stick to the plan.

Your goals should always continue to get bigger and bigger. There's never a moment when you arrive. Your target is a moving, changing, evolving mechanism that always keeps you moving forward. Even when you become the best in the world, there's still more to chase.

I'm sure you've heard the phrase, *Move it or lose it*. That couldn't be more relevant here. Once we stop moving, we die inside. You've seen it a million times with people who are on top of the world for a second and then disappear. That's because once you feel that you've arrived, you lose your hunger. Not you and I. Our target is a moving one, so we'll always be chasing. This is incredible because we've grown to enjoy the chase the most.

Despite all of this, the one thing that is likely to make you doubt yourself more than anything else is negative comments on social media. As a human, you can have a million good things going on in your life, and then one bad thing happens and you focus on that. This can bring you down real quick.

It's the same with hurtful online comments. You might get tons of positive comments on a post, and then that one bad comment feels like a punch to the gut. Focusing on that is the worst thing that any of us can do for ourselves, but it's really hard to avoid.

It may sound crazy coming from me, but both consuming and sharing on social media can have a real negative impact on your mental health. I post consistently and make sure to engage with my followers, and I have to be online enough to stay in the know about what's going on, what's hot, what's happening. But other than that, I try to limit how much social media I personally consume. It's a balance and a constant struggle to stay off my phone and enjoy life while still being tapped in.

Think about how you're balancing your time between consuming social media versus posting and sharing your own content and engaging with your followers. It's easy to fall into the habit of watching other people on social media all day long instead of focusing on what you're doing. Why not spend that time creating and posting, instead? It'll help you reach your goals faster, and it's better for your mental health, too.

Posting your own stuff almost always means getting negative comments, though. Most of the time, it's easy enough for me to take negative comments with a grain of salt. I've been dealing with professional critics as well as all kinds of jokers who think they know better than me for years. But I know that these comments tear at a lot of people, especially if they're about your appearance or something that you're already feeling insecure about. I get that. I feel it sometimes, too. Different criticisms hit me at different times, depending on my mood and what's going on with me that day.

When I first started getting active on TikTok, it was unique from other apps in that it felt really positive. It was like the twilight zone of social media, and I honestly don't know exactly why. The initial TikTok community was just supportive, kind, and super tight-knit. People on there were happy that they had someone to relate to or talk to. We were TikTokers, a group of people who were all on the same wavelength. I was so grateful that they embraced me early on as a part of that community.

It's exciting to see how much the platform has grown, but an unfortunate side effect is that it's become more like other social media apps. Now every single post will get at least some negative comments. There's no escaping it. Unfortunately, it's just a part of the social media algorithm.

There's no advice I can give you that will alleviate the pain when someone criticizes or straight up attacks you online. It's hurtful for everyone. Corny as it may sound, I try to remind myself in these moments that all this hate is coming from someone who's really insecure with themselves. How low do you have to feel to go onto someone's page and say something mean? These people are just trying to make other people feel the same way they do.

I also think about the fact that I have literally never met someone who posts negative comments online, and for sure not someone I respect or would want to spend time with. If you're one of those people who does this to me or to anybody else, seriously, stop. You're not going to make yourself any happier or more successful by tearing someone else down.

On the flip side, there's a big difference between ugly comments that have no value and the type of criticism that you can learn from. There are even times when a joke or a mean comment does end up having some validity to it. It takes a lot to see past the fact that someone is trying to bring you down and ask yourself whether or not they have a point, but it's worth it if you can use this information to improve yourself at anything you do.

I've always made it a point to listen to critics with an open mind and hear what they have to say. I have picked up on some things that were useful. After I got so much grief for using auto-tune on my first album, I made sure not to use any on my next one. People were able to see that it had been a choice the first time around, not a crutch.

I also look through the comments that people have posted on my music videos on YouTube to see what my fans like and what they don't like. This doesn't mean that I take everything people say into account. A lot of it can be written off as hate. But I have learned some valuable things, too.

For example, people noticed early on that it didn't look as if I was really singing in my music videos. I used to just lip-synch because I knew that was what most artists did. But when you actually sing the song while you're filming on set, it does look way more authentic. So all the haters out there who were criticizing me for lip-synching really helped me out.

>> The route to your success lies in your routine. Don't let anything or anybody knock you off that path.

On the positive side, I also noticed that a lot of people commented saying how much they loved it when I danced in my videos. I've experimented with all different types of videos over the years, and I love to mix it up, but those comments told me how much my audience really just wants to see me dance. So I don't go any other route now unless I'm making a video for a ballad and it wouldn't make sense for me to be dancing at all.

The most important thing is that you use any criticism you face, online or off, to make yourself better, instead of letting it stop you or dim your confidence. This leads me right back to where I started, because the best way I've found to do this is by setting a routine that I do not let myself veer from. The route to your success lies in your routine. Don't let anything or anybody knock you off that path.

4

SUCCESS IS
FOR RENT.

« »

YOU'LL NEVER PAY IT OFF.

When I was eleven years old, I started entering myself in singing competitions all around South Florida. Some of them were held at performing arts camps or schools. Others took place at malls or other public spaces. Nearly all of them offered a cash prize or the opportunity for the winner to meet with a talent agent or other music industry executive, or both. Some even rewarded the winner with free time in a music studio to record their songs. I was pumped to win and receive any and all of these prizes. But more important, I was sure that one of these competitions would end up being the big break I'd been waiting for that would launch me into superstardom.

The first show I competed in was held in a small local theater that was packed with the parents of all the kids from my performing arts camp. I was feeling confident in my skills, but as I stood backstage peeking out from behind the curtain at the crowd, I suddenly got nervous. Looking back, I don't really know why I was so scared. There probably weren't that many more people in the audience than there were at our weekly family parties, and I had never been nervous about singing in front of them. But these people were strangers, and out of nowhere, I panicked.

It's hard to explain, because I knew I was a great singer, but for the first time, I was completely overtaken by stage fright. Every bone and muscle in my body were frozen, and I started trembling a little bit. I was so nervous that at first I actually refused to go onstage.

"I can't go out there," I told my mom, who was waiting backstage with me. "There's people out there!"

I planted my feet on the floor backstage and probably would've stayed there all night if the theater's security guard hadn't physically picked me up and carried me out onto the stage himself. Hell, I might still be frozen to that spot right now! But once I was on the stage, I felt the energy of the audience, and I was totally fine. It was as if I had just needed their energy to get me going.

With my nerves gone just as fast as they'd appeared, I started singing Michael Jackson's "Ben." It was a simple ballad from the Jackson 5 days that showed off Michael's impressive vocals. I knew that it would do the same thing for my own.

The rest, as they say, is history. I won that first talent show and pretty much every one after that. My go-to songs were "Ben," "I Believe I Can Fly," and pretty much anything by Tevin Campbell. Sometimes I added a few dance moves, but mostly I just sang, showing off my voice to the crowd.

I loved performing. It was a massive high to be the guy who owned the room whenever I was on the stage. I soaked up the audience's energy, and it felt amazing to witness their reactions when I showed off my vocal range. And, yeah, I loved the feeling of winning and the idea of gaining a little local fame for being good at something. Really good.

It may surprise you to hear this, but I still suffer from stage fright to this day. I realized early on that practice was the only cure. The more I rehearsed, the less nervous I was. So as you can imagine, practice became my best friend. Even now, I have to continue to prepare at the same level in order to keep my stage fright at bay.

Before each talent competition, I rehearsed like a maniac. For hours and hours and hours, I stood in front of the mirror in my bedroom singing my little heart out, perfecting each note and vocal run. If I was planning to sing a more up-tempo song and add a few dance moves, I practiced them relentlessly, too. That work paid off every time when they announced my name as the winner.

Of course, I loved the prizes, too. I used the time I received in the recording studio to make demos, and instead of splurging, I saved my prize money for basic necessities. It felt good to be able to contribute to my family in a small way. Plus, it wasn't really an option. Lunch at my school cost a dollar fifty, and my dad always gave me seventy-five cents. It was on me to figure the rest out myself, and now it was no longer a struggle.

From that young age on, I was weirdly independent. I signed up for most of those talent shows on my own, sometimes without even telling my parents. They were the opposite of stage parents; they never would have dreamed of pushing me to compete. I was just a kid. But when they were able to attend my competitions, or when I came home and told them that I'd won yet again, they were super proud of me and always encouraged me to keep going.

Every time I won a chance to meet with a talent agent or record executive, I was sure that it was going to be my big break. *This is it,* I thought. *This will be the moment when all my hard work pays off, and I land a record deal.*

When one meeting didn't lead anywhere, I was always positive that the next one would. Nothing could dim my confidence. But, competition after competition, win after win, meeting after meeting, it never happened. Looking back, I can't even tell you *why* those meetings never went anywhere. I just know that they didn't.

This didn't deter me, though. Not for a second. It sounds arrogant, but I had zero doubt that one day I would be famous and successful. I can't even explain it. I just *knew* that success and superstardom were waiting around the corner for me. I wasn't going to let anything stop me from eventually rounding that corner.

Now I can see that I was manifesting my dreams by believing so strongly that this was my future. There's a big difference between just saying the words as you hope for the best and truly believing in your heart. For me, it was all or nothing.

> There's a big difference between just saying the words as you hope for the best and truly believing in your heart. For me, it was all or nothing.

« »

Soon after I arrived in New York City for college, I set my sights on *Showtime at the Apollo*. Yes, I was already a pretty busy guy between my classwork, songwriting, and now this competition. In case you haven't noticed, that's the norm for me.

If you're not familiar with the show, let me set the scene for you a little bit. The original *Showtime at the Apollo* was called *Apollo Amateur Night*. It was a live weekly talent show at New York City's Apollo

Theater, a landmark theater in Harlem that had started running way back in 1934. In the 1980s and through the early 2000s, networks began airing a television version of *Showtime at the Apollo*. It was like the original *American Idol* for Black folks.

At the Apollo, there was no panel of judges. The show was famous for discovering new talent and for showcasing the extremely vocal and opinionated audience. The winner each night was based entirely on the audience's response. Then that winner came back and competed against other winners each week until a grand prize winner was announced at the end of the season.

The thing that made *Showtime at the Apollo* so unique was that the crowd did not hesitate to boo artists off the stage if they didn't like someone's act. The audience didn't care how old or young you were or how much of your heart you were pouring into your performance. If they weren't impressed with you, they did not hold back. Sometimes they gave people only a second or two before they started booing. Let me tell you, the vibe in that theater was harsh.

That audience at the Apollo held every competitor's fate in their hands. And they didn't just boo off the acts that were obviously a total joke, either. They booed off plenty of people who were good, too! Luther Vandross, James Brown, and a *thirteen-year-old* Lauryn Hill are just a few of the people who've gotten booed at the Apollo.

When I passed the audition and made it onto the show, I was nervous. This was the same level of stage fright I'd experienced at that first singing competition almost a decade earlier. But this time, I wasn't performing for my family or a friendly audience of 200 or so people in South Florida. This was a huge crowd of more than 1,500 people. I had no idea what to expect from the audience, but I assumed they were looking for any possible excuse to boo me right off the stage.

Backstage before my first performance, I was sweating. It was tempting to take off the blazer I was wearing over a wifebeater with some baggy, ripped jeans. The idea of getting booed was incredibly nerve-wracking. That would not be a good look.

On the other hand, if I won, it would be my crack at stardom. No more college. (Sorry, Ma.) No more auditions. No more passing around my demo at clubs, desperately trying to be taken seriously. Instead, I'd have an actual record deal and tours and fans and a big, fat checkbook. I'd be able to touch the whole world with my music the way I'd always wanted to.

So I took a big breath to calm my nerves and walked out onstage to sing "Love," by Musiq Soulchild. This was in 2006 during my neo-soul phase, and that was one of my go-to songs for auditions.

To my relief, I didn't hear a single boo. In fact, the audience responded positively to me right away. They cheered when I executed a few vocal runs, and when I finished, some of them even got on their feet. I knew I had smashed it.

I was nervous every night when I went back and competed against another winner at the Apollo, but I managed to come out on top each time. I received cheers and standing ovations instead of boos, and I left the theater a winner again and again. It felt amazing, and when I was named the grand prize winner at the end of the season, I knew that this was it. I had finally made it.

And then . . . nothing happened.

What in the world was going on? Where were the media who were supposed to be chasing after me? Where was my record deal? Where were the fans? It seemed as if somehow no one outside of my inner circle of friends and family even cared that I had won the entire season. How was that possible?

Life has a way of humbling you. It brings you all the way down. This was a humbling and pivotal moment for me. I went from thinking

I'd be able to quit college immediately, sign a deal, and gain legions of fans, to wondering whether I was actually on the wrong path.

This was when I started auditioning for Broadway. Of course, a career on Broadway would be a privilege in itself, and it would also bring in some money, which I never really had. But I'm so grateful that I didn't veer from pursuing my dream for long.

Although my experience at the Apollo was disappointing, it was also validating. I had always believed in myself, and although it hadn't gone the way I had expected, I now had proof that my dreams were real. One of the toughest crowds in the world had responded to me in a positive way—not just once as some fluke, but over and over again. I could really make this happen. I couldn't give up now. I just had to find another way in.

That was when I realized a fundamental truth about chasing down my dream: I had to do it by myself. Nobody was going to come along and hand me a career or even an opportunity. If winning a huge competition like *Showtime at the Apollo* wasn't going to do it for me, then nothing ever would.

>> That was when I realized a fundamental truth about chasing down my dream: I had to do it by myself. Nobody was going to come along and hand me a career or even an opportunity.

There's a lesson here for anyone who's trying to break into the music industry, but it applies to you no matter what it is that you want to accomplish in life. There is no such thing as a big break. No one outside of you is going to forge your path or make things happen for you. That's on you. And it won't happen overnight or with one win or one success or even one number one hit. It takes a lifetime of working and striving and grinding and reinventing yourself again and again and again to find any kind of lasting success.

The same thing goes for hitting big on social media. A lot of people think that if they can create one video that goes viral, they'll have "made it." A viral video is great, no doubt. But, again, the real question is, how are you going to *stay* viral?

Success is a long-term commitment. It's about being able to continue capturing people's hearts and minds so you can become a part of their everyday lives over multiple years—and in my case, multiple decades. If you can do that, you're golden.

I like to say that success is borrowed. You can rent it, but you can never really own success. At this point in my life, I own a lot of nice things, but I never fool myself for a minute into believing that I own my success as an artist. I've got to keep paying that rent every month, just like everybody else.

Likewise, just when you think you've had your "big break," your rent is going to come up due. The world moves on fast. Nobody cares what you did back in the day. Hell, they don't even care what you did yesterday. They're already on to the next thing.

So what's the secret to success? Putting in the work every day to become the very best that you can be. One step at a time. One day at a time. Repeated over and over (and over) again.

<< >>

When "Whatcha Say" made it to number one, it felt completely surreal. That night, my family and I were eating at Friday's. (I told y'all. Your boy is mainstream.) All of these local fans started coming up to the table to say hi or to grab a picture with me. My parents were so proud of me that my mom couldn't stop herself from bursting into tears right there at the table.

For an artist's first single to become a number one hit is less likely than being struck by lightning seven times. That's a real stat. And for me, it didn't happen by chance like a stroke of lightning, either. Nothing in my career has happened by accident, and that number one hit was no exception.

It was a beautiful moment, but I also knew that it was just the beginning, and I didn't want that feeling of success to ever go away. I put a ton of pressure on myself to keep the momentum going. Plus, when a new artist has such a big song right out the gate, the whole music industry starts to scrutinize them. I felt like I was under a microscope. I had made the choice to use a lot of auto-tune on "Whatcha Say," and a lot of critics were criticizing me for it, claiming that it had been a crutch and that I'd probably end up being a one-hit wonder.

First of all, you ever notice that the word "critic" comes straight from the word "criticize"? Their whole job is to find fault with things. So I try not to take that criticism to heart, but I also do my best to learn from it.

I was of two minds about these reviews. On one hand, of course the auto-tune wasn't a crutch. I knew I'd have no problem with my vocals on the next song without it. On the other hand, this all ratcheted up the pressure even more. If I couldn't follow up "Whatcha Say" with another hit, I actually *could* end up being a one-hit wonder. Trust me, nobody wanted Jason Derulo to be here today and gone tomorrow less than me.

Instead of celebrating and enjoying the success of "Whatcha Say," I was completely focused on what I was going to do next. It's hard to get one hit. I'd only done it once in my life! But two hits? The idea of having to do it all over again was intimidating. So I didn't let up. I did the only thing I knew how to do: work.

It was about a year between releasing "Whatcha Say" and putting out a full album. That period of time was all about two things: promo and recording.

When it came to promoting the song, I made the choice to focus on radio. Things are different now, but back then, the program director at each radio station decided what the station was going to play. So those were the people I needed to win over.

Sure, I always trusted my music to speak for itself. But I also knew that I had to let myself be known to solidify radio play. Think about it this way—if my song and another artist's song were at the same level, how would the station choose which one of those songs to play? It comes down to a human element, and I was going to do what it took to gain that benefit of the doubt.

Nearly every day, I flew to another city, literally traveling to almost every radio station in America and plenty in other countries, too. I had dinner with every program director, kissed their babies, made friends, and exchanged numbers. I became radio's best friend.

While I was in those towns, I performed wherever I could—in bars and on top of trucks. In Tulsa, Oklahoma, I performed with a very young Justin Bieber, who was on the same circuit promoting his first single, too.

It. Was. A. Grind. Late nights, early mornings, red-eyes, and long car rides. I barely slept, but I learned to be an amazing napper. To this day, this ability is one of my greatest gifts. Most days, I'd be sitting upright in the back of a car driving from one radio station to the next, fast asleep.

I never minded. Not for one second. This was my choice, my dream, and I was happy—honored even—to put in this work. But it was still terrible for my body and for my voice to be sleeping so little and singing so much.

During some performances, I sounded horrible. Sometimes my

voice just needed a rest, and other times I had woken up right before I had to perform. It wasn't until years later that I learned about "morning voice"—when you're asleep, even if it's in a car, your mucous membranes dry out, making your voice sound deeper and irregular. Besides creating a poor performance, singing with morning voice can irritate the vocal cords even more. File that under things I wish I had known.

Whenever I was back home in LA, even for just a few hours, I was in the studio. Our first job was to figure out what song would be the next single. This was a group effort between J. R., me, my former manager, Frank, and the bosses at the label.

The initial plan was for my second single to be "Ridin' Solo." We knew it was a good song, but I wasn't 100 percent convinced that it was strong enough to come next. So I kept writing more and more songs—again, hundreds of them.

I wrote a fun dance song called "In My Bed," about a guy who's trying to get a girl to go home with him. We all loved it and thought, *This is the one*. Then I wrote one called "Love Hangover" that we also loved. Again, we thought, *No, this is the one*.

Remember what I said about getting feedback? Here's what I did. Every time I visited a radio station, I played both songs for the program director and asked them which one they liked more. I've learned that you can never get honest feedback by showing someone one thing or playing them one song and asking, "What do you think?" They'll never just say, "Eh, I think it stinks."

I've always gotten much more information out of people by asking them to compare two songs. Then I pay very close attention to how they respond while they're listening to the song and right after. If someone waits until the song is over and says, "That's good" or "I like it," that's *not* the vibe. That will not be a hit song. I know I'm playing someone a hit song when they get halfway through and they say, "Oh, shit!" It's only something special if people lose their minds over it.

In this case, I got a much bigger response to "In My Bed," so we were all set to release this as my next single. Then I played it for the program director at KIIS FM. "I like it," she told me, "but it's really raunchy in the chorus. Sonically, it feels like a song that's for everyone, but I don't think that kids are going to be able to join the party on this one."

I immediately knew in my gut that she was right. Plus, KIIS FM is a huge and influential station in the Los Angeles area. I needed the station to support the song. But instead of switching course and releasing "Love Hangover," I went back to the drawing board on "In My Bed." As I toyed around with the lyrics, I had the idea to create a play on words and change "In My Bed" to "In My Head."

With this small change, the lyrics became a fantasy instead of specifically referring to anything sexual. This made it less raunchy, and I think it made it a better song in general because of that play on words. It was a crazy last-minute change, but we jumped back into the studio to rerecord and then quickly released my second single— "In My Head."

After that, it really felt like my life was starting to shift. Everything kept falling into place, so quickly that it felt surreal. One week, "In My Head" was at ninety-nine on the charts. The next week it was at ninety-eight, then ninety-seven, and it just kept going. Radio play was growing precipitously, and I was gaining notoriety on a global scale.

"In My Head" became a top-ten song in many countries, including the US. To date, it has sold many millions of copies. I'm not bragging. My point here is that you can't sit back when you think you've made it big. That's not the time to rest. It's actually the time to take it up a notch and really start grinding.

>> You can't sit back when you think you've made it big. That's not the time to rest. It's actually the time to take it up a notch.

It's all good to experiment and fail when no one knows your name. And I'm not saying that you shouldn't keep taking risks once you're successful. We've already covered that. I *am* saying that you'll only shoot yourself in the foot if you follow up an initial success with nothing at all or with something that's just good enough. Now people are paying attention. Now they know who you are. And if you start to think you're invincible and half-ass your next work, they're going to be a lot less interested in your third project.

The lesson here is that you have to prepare now for when the world starts watching. Let's say one of your posts goes viral today. Are you ready to follow it up and for your new fans to do a deep dive into your other content?

In addition to being prepared, you have to make sure that you love what you create. When I have a hit song, I know that I'm gonna have to sing it over and over for years. Likewise, if you strike on social media, you'll have to keep churning out the same type of content that people now know and love you for.

This is exactly why it's so important for you to stay true to your creative vision. Not only does loving what you do every day make it easier to work hard, but you'll also be able to stand behind your product when it hits. It's a balance to create wildly while always being guided by what is truly exciting to you.

After "In My Head" we released "Ridin' Solo" as my third single, and that one hit the top ten, too. With three hit songs in a row, it definitely began to feel as if I couldn't miss. For a minute, I started to believe that I could just do whatever I wanted, and it would automatically hit big. But I was still busting my ass just as hard as ever, if not even harder. Instead of wanting to relax after that string of hits, the success just made me hungrier.

To me, that's the difference between ego and the type of confidence that's earned. Ego tells you that you're better than everyone else, so you don't have to work as hard as they do. Confidence, on the other hand, says that you know what you need to do to succeed because you've done it before. But you recognize that you have to put in the same amount of work to do it again.

My ego never had a chance to grow because I've always stayed so hungry. To this day, no matter how much success I achieve, I still want more, and I know that there's always so much room left to grow. I've done the work to win before, and I'm not afraid to do it again. It's a whole lot easier to stay grounded when you're constantly on the chase instead of thinking you've arrived.

As I said, I still don't believe that I own my success. In the back of my mind, I'm always wondering if I'll be able to pay next month's rent. I would like to say that this is based on a healthy sense of caution and not fear, but honestly, I'm scared as shit to fail. I started my career terrified, I'm terrified today, and I'll remain terrified until the end.

I always hold this simple truth in my mind: there is an end to everything, and we don't know when that end will come. None of us does. I always want to feel secure that if all of this stops today, I'll be able to persevere long enough to figure out what's next.

I will admit, though, that sometimes I take this to an extreme. My desire to win is so insatiable that you could call it an obsession, and you'd probably be right. Even today, it's as if I'd learned nothing from those early promo days. I still often go against my better judgment and push myself more than is healthy.

If I have a day off, which is really rare, I spend it in the studio. This doesn't allow for much rest or for enough separation between my work and my life. There is really no difference between the two. Most days, the only time I take a break is when I'm asleep. If I'm awake, I'm on the grind, going from one thing to the next.

I don't know if this is "wrong" or "right," but I do know that it's affected other parts of my life. In particular, my relationships have definitely suffered. It's difficult for anyone to understand my mindset, because mine isn't a normal way of living or of thinking. When it comes down to me choosing between my relationship and my work, my work will win nine times out of ten, and I'm probably being generous by saying only nine.

After being in this business for almost fifteen years, it's still a challenge to temper my ambition. But do I even want to? To keep paying the rent in an ultracompetitive industry, I have to be like a dog, relentless. I have to be obsessed. It's not for everyone, and it comes with its downsides. But if I want to continue this unique and special way of doing life, it means that, for better or worse, my work and my art will always come first.

5

STOP SHOWING OFF.

《 》

INVITE YOUR
AUDIENCE TO THE PARTY.

As my father told me, do something right the first time
and you won't have to repeat it again. My addition to
that is to truly see the beauty in everyone and everything and never be too stubborn to say "I'm sorry."

—LUKE BRYAN

Once "In My Head" became a top-five hit, no one would ever be
able to accuse Jason Derulo of being a one-hit wonder. Soon
after we released that single, my manager called me up and said simply, "You're on the Gaga tour."

I could not believe what I was hearing. There was no doubt that
Lady Gaga's worldwide Monster Ball Tour was going to be absolutely

huge. Her new album, *The Fame Monster*, already had a slew of hits, such as "Bad Romance," "Telephone," and "Alejandro." Plus, she was winning awards left and right.

With the year Gaga had just had, experiencing that rare combination of critical and commercial success, for her to ask a newcomer like me to tour with her said a lot. I had two hit singles under my belt, but I hadn't even released my first album yet. Nobody really knew who I was.

I can't stress enough how uncommon and unlikely it is for an artist with no album and only two songs on the radio to get an invitation to join the biggest pop tour in the world. And I can't possibly put into words how hyped I was to hear this news. I felt like jumping through the roof.

Gaga was amazing. Her hugely theatrical, over-the-top tour was exactly the kind of show that I wanted to headline myself one day. Everything that Gaga did was larger than life. Her sets were several stories high, and the show included crazy pyrotechnics, smoke, and even fire.

Then there were her costumes . . . On stage, Gaga wore a mechanical dress that moved on its own, a translucent nun's habit, and a bra that shot lasers. It was dope. Gaga is an artist with a capital *A*, and that's exactly how twenty-year-old me wanted to see myself, too.

On the tour, I learned so much from watching Gaga go out onstage and kill it night after night with all of this freaky, outlandish stuff, not to mention her massive talent. She was the biggest artist in the world, and that's exactly what I wanted to become. So I decided to take her lead and do some crazy, out-the-box shit, too.

At that time, when I was first coming out on the scene, I was trying to create a mysterious, smoldering musician vibe for myself both onstage and off. That was my brand—or what I was trying to establish as my brand. The thing is, though, that's not necessarily the real me.

Though my brother, Joey, would strongly disagree, in real life, I feel like I've got a chill, average Joe vibe. I love working out, and I love sports and going out for a drink as much as the next guy. I see myself as a typical guy who happens to have this very atypical life. But I didn't think that being an average Joe would help me stand out as an artist. So I pretended to be someone else.

I could be theatrical, I told myself. I could wear mesh clothes with spikes. I could shoot lasers—maybe not out of a bra, but you get the idea. It was exhausting to play this mystery-man role all the time, trying to fit in with the artist aesthetic, but I thought that was what I had to do to be successful.

I was joining Gaga's tour at the last minute to replace the initial opening act, Kid Cudi, who had just released his album *Man on the Moon: The End of Day*. After a few weeks on tour, Kid Cudi left to focus on recording his next album. At least, that's what he said. Cudi is a great artist, but Gaga's fans were rough on him. By the time he came onstage every night, the crowd had gotten hot. They had come for Gaga, and they wanted to see their girl.

Most nights on tour, the audience started chanting "Gaga" during Cudi's set. Sometimes they even booed. I had seen what had happened to Cudi, and I felt for him. It was painful to watch, and I hoped the same thing wouldn't happen to me.

When I joined the tour, I only had about six feet of stage to work with because Gaga didn't want to reveal her dope set to the audience before she went onstage. Plus, the stage was slanted at a crazy angle as part of the show's theatricality, which made dancing on that thing tricky as hell.

Let me be clear, I don't fault Gaga for any of this. It was her show. The rest of us were lucky to be a part of it. These days, I don't reveal anything about my shows beforehand, either. The element of surprise is a huge part of the show's impact. But it still cramped my Gaga-aspirational style. Here I was trying to go all out, but my dancers, all of our props, and I were crammed into that small, slanted space. This was all while I was out there looking like a fool who was trying way too hard to be someone I obviously was not.

You know what, though? I'm not mad at my young, spiked self. Early on in my career, I believed that I should constantly strive to be the most exciting, most innovative, and most spectacular performer in the world. Today, that's exactly who I am. But I wasn't there yet.

I've also learned since then that not everything is meant to be over-the-top. Working and living and creating outside of the box is great, but that doesn't automatically make the end product any better. To be better, you actually have to be *better*, not just more complicated and overblown.

My other problem was that at that point I had only released a total of two songs. I didn't have even close to enough material to fill thirty minutes. Before joining the tour, I felt sort of panicked. Where was I going to find thirty minutes' worth of songs, literally overnight?

I ended up getting the answer from none other than Whitney Houston. Bear with me here. I promise this will make sense in a minute.

At around this time, I happened to hear Whitney's version of "I Will Always Love You" on the radio. Now, we all know that Whitney was the best to ever do it. She was one of the most gifted and skilled singers to ever live, anywhere in this world, bar none. But as I was listening to her sing that day, I realized that part of Whitney's brilliance was the fact that despite her amazing voice, she kept her vocals accessible to the masses. She was able to display her otherworldly range, tone, and texture without overcomplicating her vocals. They were clear, concise, and effective.

Some singers think they need to incorporate a bunch of runs and vocal acrobatics into their songs to show off their abilities. Sure, they sound great, but this makes it impossible for their fans to sing along with them. Lord knows, I've heard plenty of girls sing along to Whitney even if they can't come close to hitting those notes. You know who you are. But that's the whole point—the best artists can sing a song in a very clean way while still connecting to their audience. Whitney knew this long before I did, but I'm glad she sent me that message exactly when I needed it most.

When I was in performing arts school, my teachers always drilled it into our heads that if a song is any good, you should be able to play it acoustically on the guitar. I've always kept this in the back of my mind while I was writing my songs. So I decided to stretch out my existing material by playing some of my songs twice.

I played each song once with the full-on sound, the same way you'd hear it on the radio, and then I stripped it way down and played it acoustically while singing my heart out. This gave me that clear, clean "Whitney effect" that I was looking for. Sometimes I even added a third rock version of the same song, or else I just did a cover to round out my thirty minutes.

This turned out to be a great solution, but it became obvious real quick that the rest of my over-the-top stage show was taking away from all the cool stuff I was doing musically in these different song renditions. Picture me up there singing a stripped-down, ballad-style version of "Whatcha Say?" all while wearing spikes and lasers that made no damn sense even with the original song. It was even more obvious now that I was trying to portray someone I was not.

I took note and changed it up, and the audience never seemed to mind. But the entire learning experience stayed with me. First of all, I learned that I'm not a mesh-outfit guy. I also discovered that I loved doing acoustic versions of my songs, and I kept them as a regular part of my live shows, even once I became the headliner with all the bells and whistles. On tour, I slow "Talk Dirty" all the way down and sing it out clean and clear, and let me tell y'all—it's pretty sweet.

Most important, I learned that it was more beneficial for me to start with the fundamentals if I wanted to build on them later. Larger-than-life stage performances, complex vocal runs, and elaborate outfits are nice. But they're the sundae, or even just the cherry on top of the sundae. They're not the main ingredients.

« »

In January 2020, I had just barely started using TikTok, and I mostly approached it the same way I had every other social media app. I admit, I wasn't really about social media at the time. I knew that I had to be on there to keep up with the times and to meet my goals, but I struggled with feeling fake and forced whenever I posted online.

Typing out my thoughts and sharing them on Twitter was not my thing, and flashing what I had on Instagram didn't feel organic to me, either. So I did what many artists do, which was to post about my music just enough to get by, but not nearly enough to make a real impact.

At first, it was the same for me with TikTok. In early 2020, Roddy Ricch's song "The Box" (and videos set to it) were blowing up on the platform. I jumped on the trend and posted a video of me working out with the song playing in the background. In the video, I'm doing some muscle-ups (which are pull-ups followed by a dip), all while looking stone-faced and focused, like that brooding pop star I was still trying to be. The video got a decent response, but nothing major.

This was basically how I used social media at the time. It was all about reinforcing my sultry artist image. I wasn't necessarily trying to be inauthentic, but my posts were staged, and my attitude was more "watch me" than "join me." I was trying to impress my audience instead of connecting with them, just like a singer showing off with a bunch of complex vocal runs.

Just a couple of months later, the pandemic hit. Like everyone else, I was stuck at home. But unlike most people, I was thrilled. Don't get me wrong—it was horrible to see what was happening in the world, and I felt for everyone who was suffering, especially those who lost someone they love. I had a slew of shows planned for the rest of 2020, and it was a huge disappointment to have to cancel every last one of them. But I always try to keep it positive, and for me, being stuck at home for a time came as a huge relief.

At that point, I had been touring and promoting so much that I had completely forgotten what it was like to be at home. Ever since that first promo tour for "Whatcha Say" a full decade before, I had been on a plane almost every single day—this time going from one show to the next. No exaggeration. In 2019, I was at home for sixty days out of the entire year. Even when I *was* home, I always had a show that I was preparing for just around the corner.

Going from that kind of pace to being at home for months on end was incredible. I was able to slow down and enjoy being in my own space. When I was suddenly waking up in my own bed and making myself breakfast every morning, I was like, *Wow! This is how people live?* It felt great.

But I'm not the type to sit around all day and just chill. I started to think about what I could do with this gift of free time. I had been meaning to be more active on social media for a while, especially on TikTok, so I decided to start there.

Long before the pandemic, I was aware that my nieces and nephews and all of their friends were on the app, so one day I decided to go live to try it out and get a feel for it. Suddenly, there were a million people tapped into my life. It hit me that there were a lot more people on there than I originally thought, especially tons of young people. I remember thinking that TikTok might be a resource that I wanted to tap into, but I was too busy touring and recording at the time and didn't make it a priority.

Now, with extra time on my hands and free-flowing creativity with no place to land, I had my chance. I started playing around with creating different videos, and for the first time, I was really having fun on a social media app.

Part of the magic was the fact that TikTok was simply a better fit for me personally than other social media platforms. The most popular videos on TikTok were short and lighthearted, which is the kind of content I love and that I knew my audience would respond to. Plus, it was completely open-ended. There were challenges and viral lip synch videos on TikTok that were fun to participate in, but I could also post whatever I wanted. There was no strict formula, so I could push myself creatively and open my mind to experiment with entirely new types of content that I had never created or even seen before.

Rather than viewing TikTok as just a place to post, I started to think of it as a place to *play*, where I could express myself creatively and have fun and connect with my followers. Through their responses, they encouraged me to be myself and share the raw, sometimes silly, and unfiltered parts of my life.

>> Rather than viewing TikTok as just a place to post, I started to think of it as a place to *play*, where I could express myself creatively and have fun and connect with my followers.

For example, when I posted a video of myself dancing in my closet like no one was watching, it got twelve million views. No fancy setup, no supercomplicated moves. Twelve million views. Plus, that video was way more fun to make than the kind of impressive but inaccessible workout video that I had foolishly thought my audience wanted. It was just me, dancing and being stupid—being *me*—and my followers loved it. That was incredibly eye-opening.

One video led to the next video, which led to the next, which led to the next. The more I posted and the more authentic I was in those videos, the more followers I gained. Before I knew it, my TikTok account was a massive source of pride for me. It seemed as though the entire world was suddenly copying my dance moves, and before long, I was picking up roughly two or three hundred thousand followers per day. Per *day*. Even after all the hard-won successes I had built in the music industry, I had never been praised and supported for just being myself. This was it.

With my follower count increasing and all of the momentum that came along with those eyeballs, I started to feel a lot of pressure to produce new and unique videos to keep my growing fan base excited. A lot of them were just learning about me for the first time as an artist and even as a person. They only knew me as a TikToker, which was *crazy* to me. Part of me thought that if I wanted to keep them engaged, I had to blow their minds with complex content that was unlike anything they'd ever seen before.

I had already shot the first video in my Uzo series—a comic book–like alter ego storyline I built on TikTok—with my iPhone, and it had done really well. I decided to take the next one up a notch. I hired a whole crew of martial arts experts to come to my house and choreograph a humongous fight scene. We added in some comedic elements and shot it on an expensive camera. When I saw the final video, I was hyped. It looked like a scene right out of a movie.

I was super excited to share the video with my followers on TikTok and see their reactions. And then . . . it completely flopped. To me, that meant 700,000 views. Yes, that's a lot, but understand, my previous videos were getting 14 million views, 30 million views, and then . . . 700,000? How was that possible?

I had put my best foot forward with that particular video and spent so much time and energy on it. I thought it was so much bigger and better than my other videos. How could this be the one that failed?

It took flopping hard for me to realize that this "bigger is better" mentality was no truer on TikTok than it was on a stage or in a song. Those shiny, color-corrected, high-tech videos were not what my followers expected or wanted from me. To succeed, my videos had to feel organic and down-to-earth. Just as I did with my music, I had to *connect* with my followers through my posts instead of trying to impress them.

It was the Whitney effect all over again. Why hadn't I learned my lesson the first time?

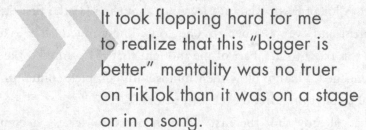

It took flopping hard for me to realize that this "bigger is better" mentality was no truer on TikTok than it was on a stage or in a song.

From then on, instead of trying to outdo myself and other creators on the platform, I focused on the existing trends and the types of content that I personally related to. Then I put my own spin on them in a way that may have been impressive but was also accessible and true to the real me. And I always made sure to encourage my followers to get in on the fun. I was finally saying "join me" instead of "watch me."

Here's an example. There was a popular TikTok challenge at the time for people to jump into their pants. It sounds strange when I put it that way, but this is the kind of lighthearted, fun shit that TikTok is all about. In most of these videos, the person started off in their skivvies while someone else held the person's pants out in front of them. Sometimes the person held their pants out in front of themselves. Then they tried to jump up and literally land in their pants. This is not an easy move to pull off!

There were some hilarious videos on TikTok of people failing miserably at this challenge and falling flat on their faces—literally. Some people did succeed in executing the jump, but I noticed that many of the ones who did had cheated a little bit. They either angled their pants down, which made it easier to land in them, or else they jumped off a piece of furniture to gain a height advantage.

I decided to embrace this challenge and elevate the trend by pulling it off in the most difficult way possible—no cheating. I had my girlfriend at the time and one of my friends stand in front of me with each of them holding on to one side of a pair of my pants. I jumped off the flat ground—with no running start or anything—and straight into the legs. It was the equivalent of pulling off a five-foot box jump and hitting the ground dressed.

We shot the video on an iPhone with no special effects or camera tricks except for slow-motion so that viewers could clearly see how masterful the move really was. The whole video took less than ten minutes to set up and execute, and it was clean, concise, and effective. To the tune of eighty-one million views.

I learned my lesson that time, no doubt.

A couple weeks later, I saw a video on TikTok where a girl bent down to pick something up off the floor, and her boyfriend tried to pat her on the butt. But this girl knew her guy too well and raised her hand up instinctively to block him. The result was a hilarious and unintentional high-five.

I cracked up watching that video because I could absolutely relate to it. That was definitely a move that I could see my girlfriend at the time pulling off. So we decided to put our own spin on it and elevate the video a little bit, but without doing anything too fancy.

I brought in my videographer, and we utilized a lot of cinematic angles, dramatic tension, and even some reaction shots from my dog, Ice. The final video played out like a showdown in the Old West, but with a butt slap instead of a gunfight. I thought it was great, but did I expect it to be my most viewed TikTok ever at that point, with more than a hundred and fifty *million* views? Hell, no. But then again, I doubt Whitney Houston ever thought she'd be best remembered for a stripped-down cover of a Dolly Parton song, either.

I think someone once said that it's not size that matters; it's how you use it. Now, I don't know about all *that,* but I do know that this saying is true at least when it comes to *the majority* of your skills. Whatever you create, think about how can you simplify it so that people can join you instead of just watching you.

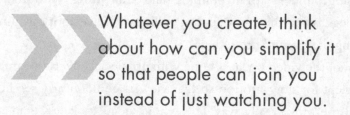

Whatever you create, think about how can you simplify it so that people can join you instead of just watching you.

I get the fact that you want to flaunt your talents. We all do. But if every moment is full of bells and whistles, you'll lose the meat and bones of the thing. What's the heart of what you're trying to convey?

Almost always, it's connection. Think about that before you add on any extras.

Allow people to join the party as well as watch. This advice holds true for any craft. You'll get a lot further by connecting with people than you will by showing off for them. Trust me—when you're that good at anything, people won't be able to keep themselves from noticing.

6

OBSTACLES ARE OPPORTUNITIES.

« »

GRAB CREATIVE
BLESSINGS IN DISGUISE.

Alright, let's do it again," my trainer called, clapping his hands together. I took a second to wipe some sweat off my forehead and then got back into position on the concrete floor. The large rehearsal studio in Broward, Florida, near Fort Lauderdale, was split into two halves—one with a hard concrete floor, and the other covered in padding. The concrete was more similar to a stage, so that's where I was practicing.

I took a breath. We were on hour six of rehearsal, and I was tired. But I was also ready to give my all to the final push. There was no music and no conversation. I was focused, and the room was silent.

With one more deep breath and a big push, I launched backward into the air, landing on my feet. Without pausing, I did it again, and then again. I was conditioning back tucks, meaning that I was doing a bunch of them back-to-back-to-back in order to build up my endurance and ensure that I could execute flawless backflips during my shows.

It was 2012, and I was about to head out on my first massive, headlining world tour. My second album, *Future History*, had just come out, and we were rehearsing for the Future History World Tour. I was pumped and ready to put on the kind of over-the-top theatrical shows I had always dreamed about. There just aren't words for how excited I was or how determined I was to put on an amazing show for my fans.

This was the most hopeful I had ever felt in my life. It seemed that with each training session, I was adding a new tool to my arsenal. The tour was going to have a ton of crazy dancing and gymnastics, and I was finally feeling ready. Acrobatics came naturally to me once I got the hang of them, and I was finding more and more ways to work them into my performance. My mind was dizzy with the new possibilities of every move I was learning, and I was visualizing ways to add more challenging—and stunning—sequences to my performance. The hours of practice were paying off, and it felt amazing.

After another ten-second break, it was time for another round. Once again, I got into position, inhaled, and launched off the ground, but this time, my foot slipped to the side a tiny bit. Things go pretty fast when you're flying backward. I was already in midair, and I froze, unable to make sense of what had happened and what I was supposed to do next.

I landed right on my head and heard a loud crack. All I could think was *Holy shit*, as I grabbed for my neck. For some reason, I had an instinct to hold it. With the help of the trainer I was working with, I got up—the second worst decision of the day after choosing to do back tucks on concrete. You're never supposed to move or get up directly after a neck or spine injury. But I was in too much pain and shock at the moment to think about any of that. I just muttered, "I'm going to the hospital," as I slowly walked to the door.

My mom was outside, waiting for me. I was getting ready to headline a massive world tour, and my checkbook was getting fatter by the day, but I was still living at my parents' house. That's how fast my world had been spinning ever since my first album came out. I didn't even have time to look for my own place.

Looking back now, I realize how insane this was. I had hit songs on the radio, I was selling out arenas, I was constantly appearing on TV, and I was even dating another pop star . . . all while living at my mom's house with a "home studio" that was just an old Dell computer in the basement. But I was too locked in to making music and riding the wave to care.

At the same time, it was nice to be around family during this crazy moment in my life. They kept me grounded, and I knew without a doubt that they cared about me because I was me, and not because of my sudden influx of money or fame.

The downside to them caring so much about me was that I knew my mom would freak out as soon as she found out that I was hurt. I walked up to her and said, real calm, "I think we should go to the hospital. I hurt my neck a bit, and I want to check it out."

I was in so much pain that I could barely walk. As my mom drove me to the hospital, every tiny bump on the road was pure hell. I desperately wanted her to slow down, but I also didn't want her to know how badly I was hurt. I just tried to breathe and keep my mouth shut despite the excruciating pain I was in.

A few hours later, after waiting and getting X-rays and whatnot, the doctor gave me the news that my neck was broken. That meant no tour, no performing, and no working out. Everything in my life suddenly ground to a screeching halt, and I was crushed.

I'm not a crier. I can probably count on my fingers the number of times I've cried in my entire life. But I definitely shed a tear in that moment. I could not believe that this was happening. How did this happen? Why me? What did I do to deserve such a freakish accident? Who breaks their neck? Besides my own disappointment, it killed me to let down the fans around the world who had bought tickets and were looking forward to seeing me perform.

Then the doctor told me that the particular break I'd sustained was called the hangman's break. It's a fracture of the second vertebrae, which is what typically kills people who are hanged. I had been a centimeter away from death and even closer to being paralyzed for the rest of my life.

I was lucky, and I was grateful that it hadn't been worse, but I was also aware of how this injury could set back or even put an end to my career. I would have to spend a couple of months in bed and seven months in a neck brace. A full recovery would take a year at minimum. The injury was devastating, but I was also determined not to let this break me or stop me.

Right away, I turned to music, and it became a saving grace. Writing music kept my spirits up during what could have been a very depressing time. I couldn't juggle a million creative projects at once anymore. I couldn't even shower without help or tie my own shoes. But I could still write songs, and for the moment, that was enough.

Instead of lying around feeling sorry for myself, I focused all of my energy on using this setback as an opportunity. As soon as I could do it safely (maybe even a tiny bit sooner if I'm being real), I started going to the gym every morning and walking on the treadmill. It wasn't much, but it was the only "workout" that I could do. So that's what I did. Then I went home and made music.

>> Instead of lying around feeling sorry for myself, I focused all of my energy on using this setback as an opportunity.

For months, I wrote song after song after song. And instead of writing sad music about how I felt inside, I wrote really happy, uplifting songs like "Talk Dirty," "Wiggle," "Trumpets," "Marry Me," and "The Other Side." I couldn't dance to these songs yet, but it made me feel good to know that other people could. I told myself that one day, I would, too.

Make no mistake—that year I spent recovering wasn't *all* good. I was in a whole world of pain from my injury, and the neck brace I had to wear for months made me feel even worse. The brace got all shoved up into my chin, and the pain kept me up at night. And it was a huge hit to my ego to be so limited and helpless, not to mention being forced to take a pause in my career at such a critical moment.

Once that year was up and I had healed, I looked back and realized that I had learned so much from this obstacle. I discovered that when you can slow your world down and focus on your craft, it opens up new levels of creativity. It's no coincidence that I wrote so many hit songs at a time when writing music was basically the only thing I could do. Focused energy is different and leads to an outcome that's on another level than when you're just finding time to create here and there.

Sometimes you can choose that zone-in time for yourself, but once in a while it gets forced on you. It may come in the form of a situation that looks like an obstacle on the outside. Or, let's be real, it might be a genuine obstacle both inside and out. But no matter what, these are still creative blessings in disguise.

Before my neck injury, when I was writing my second album,

Future History, I didn't really have that same kind of zone-in time. I worked hard on *Future History*. It's a cool album, and I got a few hits off it. But I was writing it in the middle of promoting my first album and being thrust into the limelight for the first time. As a result, the process was nothing like it had been when I was completely zoned in for my first album and then again during my recovery when I was writing my third.

It would sound corny to say that my neck injury was the best thing that's ever happened to me. In reality, that's probably going too far. But the injury did end up giving my career a huge boost instead of setting me back. When I was laid up in bed, I wrote five platinum singles. Writing them helped me keep my head in a positive space, and that album set me apart as a true artist who clearly wasn't going away anytime soon.

I also took creative risks on that album with songs like "Talk Dirty." After that, I was able to tour on a totally different scale that was even bigger and more exciting than what I had planned for the Future History Tour. I made sure not to practice backflips on concrete this time, though.

Other gifts came from that injury, too. Literally not being able to do anything for myself after being so independent for most of my life was an incredibly humbling experience. I hated it. But it also taught me what really matters in life. When all of the shows and music videos and TV appearances and radio interviews and fans suddenly go away, who is there, no matter what? It was just Mom. She was there in my corner, always ready to take care of me.

Having everything slow down like that in the middle of my early success also kept me from becoming too full of myself. Looking back now, I can see that it was really important for me that this happened, both as a person and as an artist. It taught me to block out all the celebrity noise and keep my head down and my mind right.

The lockdown during the COVID pandemic was a similar moment for me. Once I discovered the app's possibilities, I used that time to zone in on creating TikTok videos, and that's when my online audience really started growing. I relished the opportunity to experiment and express my creativity in new ways. Plus, I wasn't laid up in bed that time around, so I was able to stretch myself and create material that was physical, humorous, and musical all at the same time.

Would I have taken big creative risks and reached the same level of success if a serious injury hadn't forced me to take a beat and evaluate my career, or if I hadn't lived through a pandemic? I'll never know. What I do know is that these two forced quarantine periods reminded me that life is precious. It's also short. There's no such thing as free time, because every minute is valuable. The trick is to seize those moments of downtime when you can and use them to make yourself stronger, more focused, and more prolific.

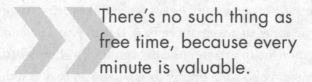

There's no such thing as free time, because every minute is valuable.

It's been ten years and a whole lot of success since my injury, and I haven't forgotten the lessons that I learned from seeing that obstacle as an opportunity. I used them to my advantage years later when I faced another situation that easily could have been seen as a setback, too.

In 2017, I released the song "Swalla," which became a platinum hit all over the world. I had hit my stride as an artist and was putting in the hours to keep the momentum going. At that point, I had been with Warner Music for almost a decade, and music industry years are like dog years. A lot of change happens in a short amount of time.

By then, the people at Warner who had "discovered" and signed me, and who had believed in me so much that they had staked their own careers on my success, had long since moved on. In fact, I had been through three completely different regimes, meaning the entire staff had left and been replaced—three different times.

Every time new staff came in, their focus was on making a name for themselves by signing new artists. That's how it works in the music industry. You don't establish yourself by helping a flagship artist maintain their success. For them, making a hit album with Jason Derulo wasn't all that exciting. I'd already been making hit albums for years. The real rewards are in discovering someone new. This meant that with each regime change, I was getting less and less energy and attention from the team.

After "Swalla" came out, it was apparently time for yet another regime change—the fourth one that I had been through at the label. This time, though, the new staff came in with their own ideas for my music. I was working on new stuff, as always, and they kept encouraging me to write songs that were more R & B than pop. These folks had come from more of an urban music background, so I understood their perspective, but I also wasn't really trying to do an R & B sound.

I was frustrated, to put it lightly. As a Black male artist, I'd been pushed into the R & B arena for years. But by this point, I thought I had enough credibility as a pop artist to stick to that genre. The fact was, this team just didn't get me. They also assigned me to work with a really young new guy in A&R (artists and repertoire). He was fine—no disrespect. But I felt that this assignment spoke to how they felt about me as an artist.

The whole situation was crazy to me because at that point I'd been the most successful artist on the label for a long time. You'd think that success would have been highly valued. I was like, *I've been keeping the lights on for a decade. I need attention to detail. I need attention, period.* The label had just given me a plaque for selling two hundred million records, and suddenly they were trying to tell me how to make my songs.

It was a deflating moment for me, no doubt. Feeling that lack of energy from the label, I wasn't in a great creative zone, either. I was supposed to release a new album under this regime called *2 Sides*. The two sides of the album were meant to reflect the two sides of my music—one with more of a pop sound and one with a more urban vibe. The idea was to release *Side 1*—a six-song EP—and then later release another six-song EP for *Side 2*.

When we released *Side 1*, I wasn't that surprised when the songs weren't hitting the same way as my previous ones. Those songs definitely reflected me being upset and not all the way in it creatively. For the first time since I was a tiny kid, I wasn't putting in as much time as I should have, and my audience could feel that lack of commitment and energy in the music.

This was a huge shot to my ego. At times like this, dark thoughts can definitely start to creep up. I'd been a successful artist for a decade. I'd had a good run. Was this a sign that my time had come and gone?

I knew by then that the best way to quiet those thoughts was for me to focus on the work and remind myself that I'd been in situations like this before with my back against the wall. If I could bounce back even stronger from a broken neck and a canceled tour, then I could also come back from this.

I spoke earlier about the difference between ego and earned confidence. In addition to knowing from experience what it takes to succeed and being willing to do it again, this is another aspect of earned confidence—knowing from experience how to recover from setbacks and being willing to do that again, too.

>> Another aspect of earned confidence—knowing from experience how to recover from setbacks and being willing to do that again, too.

I knew that the best way for me to move forward was to part ways with Warner. Then I could put my heart all the way back into my music. No matter how many hours and how much energy you put in, at the end of the day, you're only as good as your team, and my team wasn't delivering.

The problem was, I was still under contract.

My manager and I went to the label and asked them to release me from my contract. Of course, they didn't want to let me go. They may not have been as passionate about my music or my career as they used to be, but they sure were still profiting from it. It became a cantankerous situation, and it took way more time than I would have liked, but I was finally able to get out of the deal and cancel the release of *Side 2*. I'll spare you the gory details.

I was thrilled. I was finally a free agent, which felt so liberating. I could do whatever I wanted creatively. Plus, I figured that I'd easily be able to get a new deal with any label I wanted. At that point, I had sold two hundred million records. Not many artists in this world have ever done that. I assumed I could walk into any label and get whatever I wanted from them.

And that is exactly what *did not happen*.

This came as a huge shock to me. I went to a bunch of different labels, and they kept saying that I was too expensive or that I wasn't what they were looking for at the moment. I was up against the exact same obstacles as at Warner! None of the big boys wanted to pay to play. Signing an established artist like me was an investment. I knew that I came with a price, but I thought that by then I had proven I was worth it.

No, they wanted to discover someone new who they wouldn't have to pay a premium for. But to me, it didn't seem possible. Not many artists had done what I had in the entire history of music. And no one wanted to sign me? I truly didn't understand.

I hope you know me well enough by now to know that I was not going to let this stop me. Not for one minute. If I was only as good as my team, then I would just be my own team. I decided that I was going to do it on my own.

Now I know that this was another opportunity disguised as an obstacle. At this point, the music industry (along with the world as a whole) was a completely different place than it had been back when I'd first signed with Warner. Between YouTube, Spotify, and social media, artists weren't as dependent on record labels as they used to be, although most big artists were still signed to a label. I saw the opportunity to be independent, and I decided to grab it.

By this point, I had already found my rhythm on TikTok. There was a viral dance challenge going around that caught my attention. A teenager from New Zealand named Josh Nanai, who went by Jawsh 685, had created a cool beat. Pretty soon, there were fifty-five million unique videos on TikTok using the beat to showcase users' heritage and their traditional national costumes. It was incredible, and I knew that I could write a really dope song with that beat.

I reached out to Josh and told him, "Yo, I love your track. Do you want to collaborate on something?" He was hyped about the idea of working together, so I told him that I'd write a song with his beat that would work for radio. Frank, my manager at the time, and I stayed in touch with Josh, and let him know that once we had a song, we'd find the right deal for him at a label that would be excited to have him, and that we'd create a magical record to release out into the world. Josh and I talked a lot, and the excitement level in our conversations was through the roof. Although we didn't have a formal deal, our enthusiasm for working together was crystal clear—and I was so excited to start working on the song, I went straight to work.

For some reason, "Savage Love" was one of my more difficult songs to write. I had to rewrite that hook seven or eight times to get it exactly right. But I wanted the song to be perfect. Once I felt that it was, I jumped through hoops to find a great deal for it at the right label.

I called up Josh to give him the good news, but he wasn't answering. I called and called, and finally got a response: "Talk to our lawyers." Turns out, Josh had made a deal for the beat with Columbia Records.

To say I was bummed would be an understatement. I was devastated. I had been particularly obsessive with this song, and I thought it was a hit. I wanted Josh to hear it. More than anything, I was eager for the *world* to hear what we had created. I was proud of the song and hated the idea of shelving it. Even if it didn't go on to become a huge success, if people heard the song, it would at least make me feel better to know that all that work hadn't been for nothing. And now the label I had signed for the song was backing out of our agreement because of Josh's new deal with Columbia.

I told my manager that I wanted to just put the song out myself, but he warned me not to. "You can't do that," he told me. "They already have a deal with Columbia for the beat. They'll put a big artist on it, and you'll never be able to compete without a label."

Plus, he assured me, Columbia would just take down my song. They couldn't sue me because I wasn't even trying to make money off it. I wasn't selling the song. But they could still force me to take it down because the beat was now technically their property.

This was an obstacle within the obstacle of not having a label of my own. I had always trusted my manager, but this time, my gut said that he was wrong. Columbia may have had a deal for the beat, but I had something that they didn't—a hit song, ready to go. I decided to take my chances.

Right away, "Savage Love" started to go viral. Then it started to go superviral. As predicted, Columbia went crazy trying to get it taken down. They were sending cease-and-desist letters and the whole nine. But at that point, "Savage Love" was everywhere. There was no stopping the monster, and I couldn't have taken it down if I'd tried. (I'll be real with you, though: I didn't try.)

Looking back, I certainly don't fault Josh for any of this. He was coming up and wanted to get the best possible deal for himself, and Columbia is one of the biggest labels in the world. For all I know, they had no idea that I was already working on a song with Josh's beat.

I also remember what it was like to be that young artist, trying like hell to make money from my music. It wasn't until I actually started to succeed in this business that I even realized how messed up it was that I hadn't gotten paid for so much of the work I'd done for other artists early on. At the time, I was just so grateful for the opportunities. But songwriters do often get a raw deal, and Josh wasn't going to let that happen to him. I have no hard feelings about that.

Like clockwork, though, Columbia called and said the label wanted to make a deal with me for the song. Goodbye, obstacle number one. But instead of jumping at the deal, I was like, "Meh, we're good." We kept Columbia on ice for a couple of weeks, but they were persistent, so we finally ended up making a deal for the song after it had already blown up. Basically, the label had a layup. Of course, when Columbia officially released it as "Savage Love (Laxed—Siren Beat)" it was huge.

A few months later, we released a new version of the song with

BTS, and after that, the song went straight to number one on the Billboard charts. To date, the BTS collab has over a hundred million streams. The original version that I sang and wrote has more than a billion.

Not only did it feel amazing to have another number one hit under my belt, but this made me one of the only solo artists to have number one pop hits across three decades—the 2000s, the 2010s, and the 2020s. All of a sudden, every label was trying to sign me. Good-bye, obstacle number two! After all those passes, we suddenly found ourselves in the middle of a massive bidding war. But I surprised everyone when I didn't take a single one of those deals.

It didn't feel good for these labels to suddenly want me when they hadn't believed in me just a few months before. I didn't need a fair-weather record label that was trying to join the party now that I had a new hit song and my career was blowing up more than ever. The experience with "Savage Love" showed me that I didn't actually need a record label at all. If I was going to sign, it was going to be with a label that fully believed in and supported me and my creative vision and would invest as much energy and time and thoughtfulness in my career as I did.

I decided to bide my time and keep putting out more songs by myself. One of them, "Take You Dancing," went platinum, which was a huge deal for an independent artist. That year, I was a top-ten streaming artist, which was an even bigger deal for an independent artist. I'm so glad I grabbed those opportunities disguised as obstacles and didn't let them stop me.

A few months later, I did end up signing with Atlantic Records because it felt like the right fit for me at the right time. It's a fantastic label, and it's huge, but the label doesn't have any other artist on its roster quite like me. I knew that a lot of cool collaborations would funnel to me because I have a wider range than some of the other pop stars on the label. Best and most important of all, my deal with Atlantic is a fifty-fifty partnership, and I own my own masters, meaning that the copyrights to my recordings belong to me. I'm able to remain independent in the ways that truly matter.

« »

Sometimes when you're facing an obstacle, the only thing you can do is show up. I've performed in a neck brace, an arm sling, and a cast. I've even performed on crutches. Half of the battle is just getting there. But at the end of the day, you can't let your audience down. I never forget that people save up their hard-earned money to buy a ticket because they want to see me perform. I'm beyond honored. That audience and I have an undeniable bond with one another. I always show up for them.

I show up for me, too. When things get hard, I think back to the time when I was a kid with a dream, wearing headphones that worked only on one side, singing and dancing my way to the bus stop as though the entire street was my stage. That kid would have done anything to be in my place right now—*anything*! I never want to let him down, either.

This is why I treat most endeavors in my life as a battle—from the early morning gym sessions when I don't feel like working out to the eight-hour rehearsals when I don't feel like dancing, my next business deal when I don't feel like talking, and posting content regularly when my life feels way too chaotic for me to even think.

In these moments, I focus on simply showing up. Did I wake up on time? Did I have a good-enough workout? Was I attentive during rehearsal? Did I shoot three pieces of content today? Did I eat right? Then that's good enough.

Trust me—there are a lot of mornings when I have to get up early after only a couple hours of sleep, and I want to stay in bed more than anything. In those moments, I practice separating my mind from my body. People will tell you that your mind and body are one, but this leads us to allow our bodies to make choices for us, and we all know that they don't always make the best decisions! *Oh, the body is tired. The body doesn't feel like working out or eating healthy. Okay, then, let's scrap the plan and try again tomorrow.*

No way. My body works for my mind. No matter what, my mind is the boss and my body has to do what it says.

If it helps, make a game out of it. Imagine that your mind is the AI in a video game, and your body is just the skin that you've been given to play the game. If your mind knows what you have to do in order to get to the next level, it can instruct your body. Once you have that kind of power over yourself, that's when you start to live a life that you can fully control.

Set parameters geared toward the ultimate goal. Stick to them wholeheartedly. If I don't really want to work out, I work out. If I don't really want to post content, I post content. If I don't really want to work on another skill, I learn another skill. Win the day, every fucking time!

This is how you train yourself to become the beast that you were meant to be. See what it feels like to win, and get used to it. Do not take the small things lightly, because that shit's not light. Every day counts, and it's your mindset that has to change first, above all else.

At least show up, and once you get there, you can figure the rest out. It usually ends up going way smoother than you had imagined. And once you get used to showing up, it becomes natural. It's that consistency and change of mindset that will get you to work on your craft more and force you to be a better version of yourself. You have to be willing to do the work that nobody else would. That's how you'll begin to set yourself apart.

>> You have to be willing to do the work that nobody else would. That's how you'll begin to set yourself apart.

You getting this book proves to me how bad you want it. I'm here to tell you about my story, my dreams, and my failures so that you can gain the success you actually deserve. And, hell, maybe I can help you can make fewer mistakes on your journey than I did.

Thanks to all of the obstacles I've faced, I've gone through a complete recalibration of my career, and it's led me to more success than ever. In fact, I'll go as far as to say that if it weren't for my neck injury, my struggles with Warner, and the issues surrounding "Savage Love," I probably wouldn't have reached the levels of success that I am fully enjoying today.

Even if it's hard for you to see your struggles in a positive light, if you continue to focus on you and on doing your best at whatever it is you do, I have no doubt that you will discover an opportunity or two along the way. Most likely, they will be the ones that you never would have found otherwise.

7

DECIDE WHAT IS IMPORTANT TO YOU.

« »

THEN CONNECT IT TO HOW YOU SPEND YOUR TIME.

Your potential is greater than what you
believe you're capable of. Keep going.
If it were easy, everyone would do it.

— ZEDD

The whole point of my writing this book is to help you become the best possible version of *you*. And the simple truth is that you can't become that person if your body isn't in its best possible shape, too. Being in good physical shape isn't just about looking good— although, I won't lie, looking good never hurt anybody. More important, though, no matter what you do or what type of art you want to create, your body is your main instrument. You can't create your best work if you're tired or feeling down on yourself.

When you feel your best, you are your best, and that is exactly what I want to help you achieve. The reality, though, is that no one can decide what works best for you except you. On the road to finding what works best for me, there have been many, many variations. From wearing garbage bags to make me sweat more when I went running in the Florida sun to trying out super-restrictive diets and compromising way too much on sleep, I have seriously tried it all.

After all of this research and experimentation, my most important takeaway isn't a specific regimen that worked, but a deep understanding of what I want from my body and mind. It was all a process in getting to know myself and how I wanted to feel. That was an invaluable journey for me, and it will be for you, too.

I've been working out since I was a kid, and if I hadn't developed those habits so young, I have no doubt that I'd be out of shape and overweight right now. That's because I come from a family that loves food! Food is a huge part of the Haitian culture, and growing up, we were always celebrating some holiday or somebody's birthday with . . . you guessed it, food.

It was food, food, food all the time. For every birthday and family party, each one of my aunties would cook some amazing Haitian dish, and most of them included a lot of rice and other starches. I loved all of it, and I'm a foodie to this day, but I also knew from a young age that I had to find a way to balance it all out.

I wish it wasn't the case, but the truth is there's really no way to balance out eating badly with exercise—even with a crazy amount of exercise. The sad truth is that exercise is only 10 percent of the battle when it comes to getting and staying in shape. The other 90 percent is what you eat.

>> I wish it wasn't the case, but the truth is there's really no way to balance out eating badly with exercise—even with a crazy amount of exercise.

To stay fit, your diet is the foundation, and exercise is like the icing on the cake. It's taken me years of experimenting with pretty much every food and exercise plan you can imagine to figure out what works for me and how to find a balance. For me personally, I feel my best when I'm a very specific size and weight, but that's a tough state to maintain. I tend to fluctuate up and down if I'm not careful.

Most of the time, I'm careful. But many, many times, like everybody else, I say, *Fuck it*, and I fall off the wagon, so to speak. It's like a yo-yo. I let it go, and then I tell myself, *Enough is enough, it's time to get back on the shit*, and then I snap myself back into shape.

Wellness is the one area of my life where I do not apply my all-or-nothing mentality. I want to eat good food, have a few drinks, and enjoy my life without feeling as though I'm punishing myself all the time. There will for sure be times when you fall off that wagon, too, and that's okay. Just make sure you reel it back in before too long. You've done it before, and you can do it again. I know that for a fact because I have, too.

In my search to find the right balance, I've tried a lot of different things, ranging from plans that are based on common sense to ones that are completely out there, and pretty much everything in between. I followed a vegan diet for about a year and a half on two separate occasions. I still believe that being vegan is the healthiest option for longevity and overall health. The first time I did it, though, I noticed that my stomach was getting a little bigger and my arms were getting a little smaller. That wasn't a good look for me.

I went back to eating meat for a while, and then after a beat I decided to try being vegan again. This time, I focused more on making sure that I was getting enough protein. This worked better, but I was also touring around the world constantly, and I found myself in so many places that didn't have the food that I needed. In a lot of countries, the only vegan food they have is lettuce—so I ended up being hungry all the time, which was terrible for my health and for my performance onstage. Eventually, I caved.

I still maintain at least one day a week without eating any meat. My whole family does this as a sacrifice to God. Many people around the world give up meat at certain times of the year, but we do it year-round as a constant reminder.

After I gave up veganism—which I would love to get back to, by the way—I focused on eating more protein to get me in the best possible shape. For a while, I started every day with a salmon smoothie made with canned salmon blended with hot sauce. Yeah, you read that right. I know it sounds disgusting, and it absolutely was, but I also got shredded with those smoothies.

Your body doesn't have to work so hard to break down food that's already blended up. Your muscles just absorb that protein. The best part was, it didn't even matter what else I ate during the day. I stayed lean and ripped as long as I started my day with that nasty smoothie.

The whole not-chewing thing is also the reason bone broth is such a lifesaver. I've tried a bone broth diet, where I ate nothing all day but bone broth and then had salmon and veggies for dinner. This worked really well, too, but, like veganism, I had to be at home to maintain the diet.

It took a while for me to find a diet that kept me in great shape and was conducive to my lifestyle. For the past few years, I've been doing my own form of intermittent fasting. There is no one plan that's a fit for everyone, but this works well for me. Other people find that having six small meals throughout the day works best for them. You have to find what's right for you. It's all about calories in and calories out, so experiment to find a sustainable way for you to live without the yo-yo of weight gain and weight loss every month.

As it is, I find that if I basically fast throughout the day, I can have an awesome dinner without having to be super strict about what I eat at that one meal. Sort of reminds me of getting that one free meal a day back at Warner. Maybe that's when I trained my body to thrive that way.

To me, dinner is sacred. It's usually the time when you can break bread with the people you care about and unwind after a long day. If you have to keep it to broiled chicken breast and three spears of asparagus, it sucks the life out of how meaningful and fun a nice meal with friends or family can be. I also like to have a drink or two with dinner. So if I'm doing that and eating a big meal at night, I can't be having snacks all day, too.

At dinner, I generally let myself eat whatever I want as long as I lead with protein. I still try to eat things that are decently healthy, but I'm not strict about it. The most important thing is to maximize my protein intake so I don't lose any muscle.

During the day, I have some sort of juice or a shake. Coffee, for sure. I love ginger tea with lemon, which is great for digestion and really helps curb hunger. That's one of my best hacks. Otherwise, gum helps. The fruit water Treo also helps. I love Treo so much that I became an investor in the company. I like to have one before dinner because it manages my hunger and sometimes after, as well, when I know I shouldn't have dessert but I'm really craving it. I do have my hungry times. But I remind myself that there's no meal that tastes as good as having a six-pack feels.

You don't need to subscribe to any one diet plan as long as you put good ingredients into your body. The best diet advice that anyone can give is to lead with leafy greens and proteins that God made. Those are the best foods for our bodies, period.

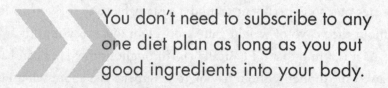

> You don't need to subscribe to any one diet plan as long as you put good ingredients into your body.

Our bodies work hard for us. We put them through sleepless nights, late nights out drinking, and stressful times. It all takes a toll. We owe it to our bodies to give them the fuel they need. We can either have an optimal day when we feel our best and crush it, or we can feel sluggish and go through the motions. A lot of this depends on how we treat our bodies.

If a food was made by humans in a lab, it's probably not what your body needs. Of course, you can still eat these things sometimes. I definitely do. I mean, have you seen my Milli Meals on TikTok? But if you want to feel and look your best, you can't have those things all the time. The trick is to find a balance that works for you so you can sustain it. Consistency is what gives us results, not trying some extreme plan and then giving up quickly.

The same exact thing goes for working out—consistency is key. You're not going to get very far working out for one week, burning yourself out, and getting right back on the couch. Even if working out is just the icing on the cake as far as your fitness goes, it's still important to exercise for energy and general wellness. Plus, who doesn't want icing on their cake?

I never know when someone in an audience is going to ask me to take my shirt off. I've got to be prepared at all times. But more important, it's a lot harder to perform onstage when I'm not in my best shape. I can either cruise through a show because I'm fit, or I can struggle through it because I'm not feeling my best.

My best shows are when I'm at my peak fitness level because there's nothing I can't do onstage. When I'm not so fit, I have to limit my shows to what I can do physically while singing at the same time. Basically, if I'm fatigued, I have to pick my own pockets. That results in a very different show from one where I'm unstoppable, and I always want to give my audience the best possible experience.

I've always loved working out, but it wasn't until after my neck injury that I really started taking it seriously. That's when it became an obsession for me. For the seven months that I was in that neck brace, I could barely move, and it drove me nuts. As soon as I had the opportunity, I started going HAM, full-throttle, crazy.

Before the accident, I weighed about 180 pounds, and when I got out of the neck brace, I was down to 163. At that point, I really started to focus on gaining muscle while staying lean. When I got back to performing in late 2012, I took the Insanity workout series with me. The Insanity workout is basically a combination of body-weight exercises and high-intensity interval training (HIIT). I was doing three hundred push-ups every single day. I did Insanity before the show, then thirty minutes of abs, then the show itself, and then more push-ups. Before long, I went from feeling as though I was wasting away in the brace to being in the best shape of my life.

Ten years later, I'm always trying to figure out how I can best myself. The age I am now is the same age that Michael Jackson was when he released the *Bad* album. I'm not even close to entertaining the idea of being over-the-hill just yet—or anytime soon. This still needs to be my peak, and I work hard to make sure that it is.

I always work out. Always. Five times a week at least. This is just maintenance for me, and I feel as if I look pretty average when I keep it to this level. My body doesn't get to an extraordinary place unless I'm doing at least two workouts a day—one cardio and one lift.

Again, that's just me. You're not competing against anyone but yourself. If you're starting from nothing, get going by doing a little bit every day, and then build from there. Try to keep one-upping yourself. If there's a sport you like, play it. If there's an activity you enjoy, do more of it. Exercising three times a week is great for your health and will give you a decent lifestyle. If you want something more, then you have to be willing to put in more and commit to working out at least five or six times a week.

Keep in mind that making time for recovery is just as important as working out. Sleep in particular is critical. It sets up your day and is such a huge part of your health and wellness. When your body has time to adequately recover, you can see and feel the difference. You don't get those gains in the gym. You've got to break down the muscles and let them recover so they come back stronger.

> Life is all about deciding what's most important to you and connecting that to how you're going to spend your time.

When I get real sleep, I always end up looking leaner and feeling better. I also spend a lot of time in the steam room and sauna and try to get massages when I can. I don't stretch nearly as much as I should, but I'm trying to get better at that as I get older.

At the end of the day, getting in shape is just like anything else that you want in life: it takes work. Sure, there are a few anomalies out there who are just born different, but most people don't get a great body or a six-pack by accident, just as they don't reach massive levels of success by accident, either. They do it by setting a goal, working their asses off, stumbling, falling, getting back up, and working some more.

Life is all about deciding what's most important to you and connecting that to how you're going to spend your time. It sounds simple because it is. It doesn't really matter what you were born with or what kind of shape you're in right now. If you decide that you want to improve yourself in any area and you're willing to work at it, there is literally nothing that can stop you from the body, the career, or the life of your dreams.

8

THOSE WHO CAN, DO.

« »

THOSE WHO CAN'T,
BECOME CRITICS.

Whatever you create, your success is always about so much more than that creation itself. It also depends on the meaning behind your work, how your audience connects to it, and whether or not they develop an authentic connection to you as an artist, a creator, and a person.

When I started to find success in the music industry, every powerful person I came across hammered it into me that success was about much more than making music—even great music. This is still true today. For an artist to really hit big, everything has to come together perfectly at once: the right song at the right time, sung by the right artist with the right voice, who knows how to connect with the masses in the right way.

That's the trifecta: song, voice, and connection. And I don't mean just connecting with people through the songs themselves, although of course that's important. I'm talking about connecting with fans on a human level so that over time they develop a deeper interest in you than just as someone who happens to sing some cool songs.

The same thing goes for social media and all other crafts. Two people with similar platforms can release the same song or identical social media posts, and they'll each hit a little different. Most likely, one will be much more successful than the other. What is the missing link between the two? It's the audience's connection to and impressions of the person behind the art. This matters more than some artists, including me at the beginning of my career, want to believe or admit.

Despite knowing all this, before my first album came out, I focused 100 percent on my music and my voice. If I'm being real, I focused on those two things more like 5,000,000 percent. Aside from borrowing my brother's clothes, I didn't put much thought into my public image—things like what I wore, how I looked, or how I presented myself to the world. I didn't have time to worry about all that because I was way too busy grinding.

I was still a kid. At nineteen, I was coming out onto the scene, and I was so hungry for the world to hear my music and discover everything I had to offer. I was a blank slate, completely impressionable, and open to anything that would keep my career rolling in the right direction.

This meant that when the "experts" stepped in to offer advice on what I should wear and how I should act to connect with fans and listeners, I was all ears. But it wasn't long before I realized that it was truly the blind leading the blind in this department. Warner Records was primarily a rock label. They knew how to help create a public image for rock musicians, but not for a pop artist like me.

Meanwhile, Joey, Henry, and Harry were still my core team. Joey may have had some nice clothes, but they knew exactly as much about real fashion and image as I did—nothing. We tried to wing it on our own the way we had back in Miami, but this time there was a much smaller margin of error. So when the so-called experts stepped in with their own ideas, I tended to listen.

The reality is, a lot of people have jobs built around an artist's success, and it's common for them to try to sow seeds of doubt in order to justify their jobs. This may sound harsh, but it's the truth. For example, look at all the awards shows out there. The entertainment industry puts a huge emphasis on nominees and winners each year, but why should we let this establishment define success? We don't need some invisible panel of judges to tell us which music is the best when the numbers don't lie.

So why do those awards shows even exist? Because . . . money. If an establishment can convince an artist that their success relies on them, then they can siphon off some of that success. The same goes for record labels, stylists, publicists, executives, you name it.

I'm not completely dissing the industry. I've worked with so many talented people in my time. But I've also learned that just because someone has a certain job title or an opinion, that's no reason to automatically trust them. I have definitely been burned a time or two by "experts." And especially as I was coming up, I found that their undue influence preyed on my insecurities more than my knowledge gaps.

I had no clue at nineteen years old how to present myself authentically or how to present myself at all. Making music was always the easy part for me. I worked hard at it, sure, but I've always felt comfortable in my own skin as a musician. Putting myself out there as a person didn't come as naturally.

The truth is, all I ever wanted to do was put my head down and make music, and that road has led to some really successful songs! Image-wise, though, I was struggling to figure it out. At first, I found giving interviews and speaking in public really difficult. I'd never had to do anything like that before and constantly second-guessed myself. Every time I spoke or moved, I asked myself, *How does a successful person walk? How does a successful person talk? How does a successful person do an interview?*

No doubt it would have been better for me to just live in the moment and enjoy the exciting ride I was on. If I could go back in time and talk to nineteen-year-old Jason Derulo, the first thing I would tell him is, "Just be yourself, man!" But I didn't know how to do that yet or even who I really was.

I had spent my entire life up until that point as a student. I had studied all kinds of music, theory, every form of dance, singing, acting, opera, Shakespeare, you name it. So that first year out, I did what I knew how to do: I studied.

This time, I studied successful people and modeled myself after them. Mind you, I'm not talking about new artists who were trying to *become* successful, the way I was. I was looking at the folks who had already achieved staying power in their careers. That's where I saw myself going, so that's where I set my path.

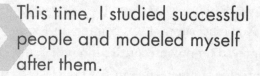

This time, I studied successful people and modeled myself after them.

I know it sounds crazy, but my number one takeaway from looking at other artists and listening to the people around me was that I had to be *weird*—that's my word, not theirs. I may be an average Joe, but a lot of other successful artists aren't. After watching them go on-stage and interact with the media and their fans, and meeting many of them offstage myself, my takeaway was that being an artist meant being mysterious. From the way they talked to the way they dressed and even the way they moved, they were eccentric in a way that I was not. But I couldn't deny the fact that being a little weird helped them stand out.

For me, I was pursuing success by any means necessary. Anything that I had to do, I was willing to do. So I looked at these artists and was like, *Okay, I guess I have to be a little weird like that, too.*

Whenever I did interviews or spoke in public, I turned on my new persona: Jason Derulo, the artist. That guy spoke softly, thought deep thoughts, and was very, very serious. I paired this new persona with a fashion sense that was . . . equally questionable. I admit, I looked goofy. The spikes and the mesh from the Gaga tour aside, what about the close-cropped hair and that chin-strap beard I was trying to rock when my first album came out?

This was a brand-new look for me. I actually still had my long braids on the original single cover for "Whatcha Say." That had been my look for so long, and I thought it worked for me. But as the song started to swell, I decided to cut my hair. A clean cut for a fresh start—or so I thought.

Seriously, please go look at the video for "Whatcha Say." No, I'm not just trying to get more views. That will drive the point home that I am trying to make here. That facial hair, my God. It's straight-up painful. The worst part is, I thought I was fly. I remember looking in the mirror after getting the chin-strap and actually thinking, *Yo, this frames my face perfectly*. I liked it so much that we reshot the cover of "Whatcha Say" to show off my new look.

Looking back now, it looks as if I was auditioning for the role of artist and put on the outfit I was wearing as some sort of experiment.

Well, it looks that way because that's exactly what I was doing! I was playing the part of a mysterious artist, but I had no clue how easy it was to see right through me. Some critics even made fun of the spikey jacket I wore in the "Ridin' Solo" video and said how derivative it was. (Note to self: No. More. Spikes.)

The truth is, no one was buying my act. In the ten years or so following the release of "Whatcha Say," I released a lot of hit songs—a *lot*. But most people *still* didn't really know who I was. Yes, I had made sure they knew my name, but they still didn't really know *me*.

Millions upon millions of people around the world were listening to my songs, singing along with them, dancing to them in the clubs, even watching my music videos . . . and the whole time, they probably wouldn't have been able to pick me out of a lineup. I can't tell you how many times I showed up for an interview at a radio station and had the interviewer say, "Oh, you look totally different from how I pictured you" or "I thought you were white!"

For almost a decade at this point, I had been making hit songs and promoting them like crazy. I did every late-night show, I performed on TV all the time, and I was selling out huge stadiums all around the globe. And these fools were out here playing my songs for their listeners with no clue who the hell I was.

Plenty of people were buying into my songs, but they weren't buying into Jason Derulo the artist or the brand. While I didn't know the reason for this disconnect exactly, I had started to become suspicious of the experts who had been trying to tell me what to wear, how to act, and who to be.

The one thing I *did not* want to do was to put all of my personal drama out there to fill the pages of random magazines or give every chat show on the planet something juicy to talk about. There were many times when I was encouraged to drop a little something to create some gossip and put my name in everyone's mouth. I knew that was what many stars did to get themselves out there in a big way, but I had no interest in any of that. Again, I was taking the road less traveled.

This brings me to the lesson of this chapter: ignore the experts. And I don't just mean the misguided industry people giving you endless notes about how to change (although please don't listen to those people, either). The "experts" in your life include anyone who tries to shape and influence you, whether they deserve that influence or not. Think about it. Has this person done what you're trying to do? If not, then they don't actually know how to do it, do they? Those who can, do. Those who can't, become critics.

Think about it. Has this person done what you're trying to do? If not, then they don't actually know how to do it, do they?

For me, the real turning point came when I was long into my career, around the "Talk Dirty" era. Yes, I had already toned down the mysterious artist vibe and gotten rid of the chin-strap and spikes. But the fake persona didn't completely go away until after I broke my neck. After that traumatic experience, I knew that if I was going to keep doing this thing, I was going to have to do it my way. I had always done things my way musically, but image-wise it was time to take the reins and be my true self.

I freed myself up to start wearing things that I actually liked and felt comfortable in instead of what everyone around me thought an artist "should" wear. Once I did this, I actually got really into fashion and was able to have fun with it. The fake chains were replaced by some real ones, and a more confident, authentic, and sexier version of me started to emerge.

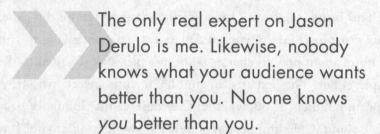

> The only real expert on Jason Derulo is me. Likewise, nobody knows what your audience wants better than you. No one knows *you* better than you.

I attribute this change to a few different things. Yes, I had stopped listening to bad advice, but I had also grown up. After I launched a very public career at a very young age, the world watched me go from a hungry, wide-eyed kid to a confident, successful man. Along the way, I got to know myself. I learned who I really was. And this made me more comfortable letting other people see the real me.

It's no coincidence that I started being my most authentic self during a time when I was focused entirely on the music and the work. That was the ship that I was meant to steer, and I didn't need the experimental facial hair or soft and sultry artist voice to do that. Anyone who had my best interests at heart would have pushed me to be authentically *that* person: the musician and performer I was and had always been.

What did I learn from all of this? The only real expert on Jason Derulo is me. Likewise, nobody knows what your audience wants better than you. No one knows *you* better than you.

There's nothing wrong with taking lessons from the people you admire, trust, and respect. But your gut is *always* the real expert when it comes to doing you. To succeed and stand out in a crowded world, trust yourself more than what anyone else tells you.

9

RESPECT THE HIVE.

« »

YOUR COPILOTS ARE AS IMPORTANT AS THE DESTINATION.

*I'm not trying to be credible,
I'm trying to be incredible.*

—DAVID GUETTA

I was in middle school when all the boy bands were popping. Groups such as NSYNC, Backstreet Boys, and 98 Degrees were dominating the charts in the US, and around the world, there were even more huge groups like 5ive and Westlife. Of course, the Jackson 5, one of my biggest influences, was like the daddy of all boy bands. It didn't take me long to wonder whether a boy band might be the "in" I needed to make it as an artist.

After me, the best singers at my school were two guys named DeAndre and Xavier—the same guy I wrote "Ridin' Solo" with years later. I talked them into starting an R & B group with me. We called ourselves JDX—Jason, DeAndre, and Xavier. Not the most creative name in the world, but it worked. I had come up with a plan for the three of us to rehearse together every day after school and start entering as many talent competitions as we could. I thought that if we worked hard enough, we'd have a real shot at mainstream success.

Who knows? Maybe we would have, but we never really got a chance to find out.

Before we took the stage for our very first competition as a group, I stood backstage with Xavier. "Where the hell is he?" I asked, pacing around like a maniac. DeAndre was nowhere to be found, and we were supposed to be the next group up to perform. To make things worse, between DeAndre and Xavier, DeAndre was by far the better singer of the two! Even though Xavier was a closer friend, he's not the friend I would have chosen to be stuck with. LOL.

I was already frustrated with both Xavier and DeAndre. Ever since we'd started the group, I had to constantly chase them down to rehearse. They were often running late or "too busy" doing something else. It felt as though it was on me to convince them to be great. They just didn't want to be heard as much as I did, and I was getting sick of dragging them along behind me.

DeAndre never showed for the competition, and I was stuck trying to make it work with Xavier. It was the first time that I didn't win one of those contests, and—not coincidentally—it was the last time that I joined a group of any kind. I've been "Ridin' Solo" from then on, and I've never looked back. It's ironic that Xavier later became one of my best friends and ended up being in the room when I was writing that very song!

I had known for years that I wasn't the same as other kids, but this was the first time I understood on a deep level how fundamentally different I was from almost anyone else around me. I'm not mad at those guys. I hope they have great lives today. But when it came to our work ethic, we were not on the same page. I'm glad we disbanded so quickly, because our group never would have worked. No matter how hard you try, you can't force someone to be great if their heart's not in it.

The fact is, there are so few people out there who are willing to grind it out all day, every day, the way I do. No surprise, a lot of the people in this tiny pool do end up becoming very successful. It's also not a coincidence that the vast majority of them do it alone. Either they start out alone, or they end up going it alone after separating from a group. The reason is that it's common in a group situation for there to be one insanely determined person who's dragging everyone else along with them. It's only natural for the person doing all of that dragging to start feeling resentful.

I've got no time for any of that drama. Ever since JDX disbanded, I've known that I had to do it by myself. By "doing it," I mean being the one with the vision, the one with the hustle, and the one putting in the countless hours of work that it takes to become the best and to stay that way.

I'll be real with you, though. It's not for the faint of heart. And I'm not just talking about music, either. This is my approach when it comes to everything I do, from the businesses I invest in to the songs I've put out, my social media posts, and every other project I sink my teeth into. There's a simple reason for this. I'd rather go down with a ship that I truly believe in than a ship that I *know* I could have built and steered and captained better on my own.

I know what I like and what I don't like, and that's usually in line with the public's tastes. In general, I'm a fan of the things that most of the world likes: pop songs, superhero movies, and McDonald's. As I mentioned before, I'm a mainstream daddy through and through. This is where being an average Joe has been an advantage for me. My tastes are usually on par with the mainstream audience. So I know that when I hold on to the reins and make a project my baby, it will most likely have wide appeal.

Not everyone has the vision or the drive or even the desire to be the one in control. Some people have a more deferential personality, but that's not me. If you're a worker bee, there's no shame in that. Just go out and be the best damn worker bee the world has ever seen. But if you do decide to hold on to them reins, hold them tight. And if you choose to hand them over, do it completely. You can't half-ass your way to fulfilling your creative vision. No one can.

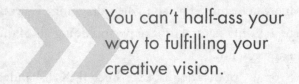

> You can't half-ass your
> way to fulfilling your
> creative vision.

If you do have a vision and you want to see it through, then you've got to be a control freak like me. If you give up control, chances are that you'll have to make compromises and spend too much time dragging other people along with you. No doubt the end product will suffer as a result.

With all of that being said, doing it by myself, even as a control freak, doesn't mean that I do it *all by myself.* I'm talking about holding on to creative control so I can make sure the project stays true to my vision. But part of being a control freak means finding the right people—the worker bees you need to fill in your hive. You cannot succeed without people you trust around you who will put their hearts and time and energy into playing their unique role to help you execute your vision.

Lucky for me, I was born in the hive. My brother and my cousins who work with me dropped everything in their own lives to help me make my dreams come true, and they've never been the least bit jealous or resentful of my success, because they know that it's their success, too. We each have our own role to play, and we all respect one another's work and unique contributions. Throughout my career, all of the people who've worked the most closely with me were either part of my family or have been in my life for so long that they might as well be family.

Case in point: Frank.

After junior high, I went to Dillard High School in Fort Lauderdale. It was a magnet school for emerging computer technology and performing arts, and it also happened to be a regional basketball powerhouse. A strange combination, I know. Although sports such as basketball never came as naturally to me as music, I loved the game and tried out for the basketball team my freshman year.

A few days later, a list was posted in the hallway of everyone who'd made the team. As I walked over, some other guys were gathered around all excited, having seen their names. There were whoops and high fives all around me. I scanned the list quickly at first, expecting to see my name, but it wasn't there. I slowed down and read it more carefully, and then checked one more time to make sure I hadn't missed it. I hadn't. My name was not listed. I hadn't made it.

Kids can be brutal. At school, I was known as a singer, and it seemed as though the guys who had made the team were taking satisfaction in seeing me fail at "their" thing. As I walked away, I heard one guy say, "Oh, you didn't make it, huh?" A round of laughs ensued, and another kid added, "Yeah, you need to go sing a song."

I felt those words. I was angry, sad, and embarrassed. That feeling of rejection was new to me, and I didn't like it one bit.

When something like this happens, you can let it crush you or you can let it propel you. It's up to you. Will you accept defeat or not? You have the reins, and you can turn yourself into the person you want to be with the right mindset and effort. The mindset has to come first.

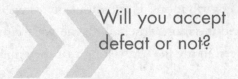

Will you accept defeat or not?

For me, those crushing moments are the ones that make me hunker down and get lost in the work so I can build myself up in a new way. I wasn't going to take this defeat lying down. I wanted to show those guys that I could do it, too. I decided that not only was I going to make the team the following year, but I was going to become a star basketball player.

I knew what it would take to get to that level, and I committed to it. For the next year, I carried a basketball with me at all times. I dribbled my way to the bus stop at 4:00 a.m., I slept with a ball in my bed, and I spent all of my free time hooping at the neighborhood court, trying to get better. I gave up most of the little bit of sleep I was already getting to improve at basketball, but I didn't care. I was serious about basketball, and when I'm serious about something, I'm unstoppable.

That summer after my freshman year, I ate, slept, and breathed music and basketball and nothing else. I woke up, spent hours singing and writing songs at home, and then I spent a few more hours at the neighborhood court before hitting the clubs at night. Most days, the same group of guys showed up at the court. We'd team off and hit it.

One day, there was a new guy there named Frank, who was older than the rest of us. He had on high socks and some shorts that were a little higher than regulation. He was basically the last guy that any of us would have picked to be on our team, but I got stuck with him. Then he came onto the court and absolutely destroyed us.

We talked after the game, and Frank told me that he had played professional basketball in Switzerland. When I explained about trying to make my high school team, he agreed to train me. Frank was in law school during the day, so we met up to practice for hours every night. He killed me every day. No matter how hard I trained, I could not beat him. And you already know how much I hate losing.

One day, I got so frustrated from losing to Frank yet again that I exploded. "This isn't even my thing!" I yelled. "I'm really a singer."

Frank just waved me away with his hand. "You can't sing, man," he said dismissively.

That was it. I was so hot, I just opened up my mouth and sang the first song that came to my mind, which was "Can We Talk," by Tevin Campbell. Frank listened in silence, holding his basketball under his arm. When I was done, he shook his head and said, "Alright, I guess you *can* sing."

Frank told me that he had some connections in the music industry and that he would help me out, and from that day on, he became a huge part of my team. At the time, though, it turned out that Frank didn't have any real connections. We figured it out together. He put in the time doing the research while I put in the time perfecting my craft. Frank is no longer my manager, but he became my mentor from that day on. We built this whole thing together, and I respect the hell out of him.

In basketball, I learned that I wasn't being aggressive enough in terms of shooting. I played defensive and always looked for the pass. Frank taught me to shoot my shot, every single time. If I missed, I'd get it back again. That was a tremendous lesson that I've carried with me throughout my life. We're always so nervous to fail, but it's the failures that give us the opportunity to win. And as soon as you start winning, people will forget that you ever messed up in the first place.

Here's something I bet you didn't know—Michael Jordan, LeBron

James, and Kobe Bryant are in the top ten of the players with the most misses of all time. That's right—misses. With Kobe coming in at number one and LeBron at number four. The point is, they always take the shot, and they wouldn't have so many wins if they didn't have all those misses. It's no coincidence that almost the entire top ten for having the most misses are in the Hall of Fame.

That summer, I met Frank at the court every evening after a full day of making music, and he'd take me through drills. As much as I wanted to play recreationally with the other kids, that training with Frank put it all in perspective for me. When you're playing recreationally, you end up taking somewhere between one and seven shots the entire game. You can put way more baskets up on your own.

I'm a creature of habit, which can be a positive or a negative thing, but it's served me well throughout my life. As you know, there was a time when I ate four bananas a day. There was another time when I had a Subway footlong sandwich every day. Even now, when I go to my favorite restaurant, Catch, in LA, I always order the same thing.

It can be fun to keep things fresh and exciting, but it helps you work toward a goal if you know what your life is going to look like the next day. You get used to doing what you have to do instead of making new decisions that might lead to a different result. Once I find what works for me, I don't deviate until it stops working. Then I find something new and commit to that. This is one of my superpowers.

>> Once I find what works for me, I don't deviate until it stops working. Then I find something new and commit to that. This is one of my superpowers.

This is how I approached basketball training. Picture me in a movie montage doing two hours of drills, drills, drills: dribbling, layups, footwork, passing, and shooting. Maybe the theme song from *Rocky* is on in the background. Then Frank and I would play one-on-one. That was the fun part, even though Frank always destroyed me. Then he'd tell me, "I'm heading home, but make sure you do your two hundred jump shots."

This was summertime in South Florida. When I say that I put in blood, sweat, and tears, I mean it literally. After another hour or more of practicing jump shots, I'd run home, shower, and change into my club "uniform." Then my brother, cousins, and I would head out to the clubs.

What's the lesson here? Start thinking about who is riding alongside you as much as where you're going. If you feel you're heading in the right direction at the right speed, doing work that is meaningful and successful, you probably already have the right people on your team. But if you feel like you're being held back or misguided, or that you're wasting time and energy dragging people up with you, chances are that it's time to cut yourself free and see what you can do on your own.

And oh yeah—of course, I ended up making the team.

10

TRUST THE DATA.

« »

CREATIVITY AND ANALYTICS
GO HAND IN HAND.

One day very early in my career, Frank came to me with a huge stack of international music charts from every genre over the past ten years. Frank is the man when it comes to data analysis and statistics. He knows every single stat about every sports star out there. I'm always telling him that if he upped his social media game, he could be a massive star. People all over the world would be blown away by his wealth of knowledge.

Anyway, back then, Frank and I sat down together and looked closely at the charts. They told me exactly how many albums different artists in all kinds of genres had sold and where their songs and albums had fallen on both the national and international charts. Seeing those numbers in black and white was incredibly eye-opening. In fact, it completely changed the way I looked at my career.

I am, and always have been, a music lover, period. I love jazz. I love R & B. I love hip-hop. I love neo-soul. I even love country music. But to succeed as an artist, I knew that I had to focus on one genre of music.

I didn't choose which genre I loved the most or which one came the most naturally to me. I chose the genre that the greatest number of people listened to, because I wanted to be the biggest artist in the world.

Notice that I said *in the world*. In the US, pop is big for sure, but hip-hop and R & B are, too. A lot of people think that rappers and hip-hop artists have the biggest bags because those genres are so hot in the US. But globally, pop is far and away the biggest genre of music. Hip-hop, R & B, and rap aren't even in the same universe.

From a young age, I knew that I didn't want to limit my audience to just the US market. I wanted to reach as many people as possible, no matter where they happened to live. When I watched Michael Jackson perform on TV, he was always in some exotic country, and I admired that cross-continental fan base and support. I imagined myself selling out arenas in Germany and Australia, and my music touching the whole world, too.

Growing up in Miami also showed me an international picture. The kids I went to school with were from all over the globe—Puerto Rico, Cuba, Jamaica, Haiti like my family, and plenty of other countries, too. I always knew there was a big world out there outside of my neighborhood and even my country, and that every corner of that world had a lot to offer. There were so many different cultures and people outside of the US that I could connect to through my music. I'd be doing myself a disservice by focusing on the US just because that's where I happened to be born.

Meanwhile, Frank had played basketball in Switzerland and had seen firsthand how big the world really was. With those charts, he presented me with simple math. There are four hundred million people in America. That's a lot of fuckers. But there are *eight billion* people in the world.

From a purely numerical perspective, focusing on the most popular music on the planet would give me a much greater chance of global success, simply because of all the different markets I could tap into. Charts don't lie. Once I understood them, I made it my goal to become not just a successful artist, but a global pop star.

Think about what kind of numbers and data and math *you* need to study in order to make it in your chosen field. People seem to forget that the entertainment industry is a business just like any other. In most businesses, the people who focus on the numbers and the data are the ones who thrive, and it's no different in a creative industry.

It's a great thing to make art, but doing it in a vacuum without paying attention to what people actually want to watch and see and hear won't get you very far. Even if you don't care about money (which I doubt is true), your art will reach more people if you focus on the data. And what's the point of making art if it never has a chance to touch people's lives?

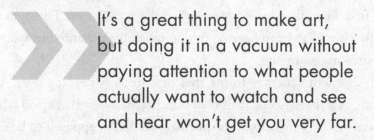

It's a great thing to make art, but doing it in a vacuum without paying attention to what people actually want to watch and see and hear won't get you very far.

Once I had my eye on the prize, I approached every aspect of my career from a global perspective. I wrote the songs that I believed would appeal to the widest possible global audience and traveled constantly, more than any other artist, to cultivate new markets in Europe, Australia, Africa, and Asia. Eventually, I became the first artist to perform in front of a mixed audience of men and women in Saudi Arabia. It was a really special, beautiful moment that never would have happened if I hadn't spent so much time and effort establishing myself as a global brand.

I'll take it a step further—I wouldn't be nearly as successful as I am today *in general* if I hadn't focused on becoming a global pop sensation, even though I'm just as good at R & B as I am at pop. In fact, it would have been much easier in some ways, and certainly more expected of me, to pursue R & B. But I had bigger goals and dreams than that.

Let's face it: I'm a Black singer, and in this country, Black singers are expected to stick to R & B or to at least start out with it. I was pushed in this direction my entire life simply because no successful Black male artist has ever started off in pop music. Think about it. Even Michael Jackson started off as a kid with the Jackson 5 doing R & B before he went on to become the "King of Pop."

Even today, everyone in the music industry insists that Black artists, especially males, have to start off in R & B and build an "urban" base first. Then they can "cross over" to the mainstream. The lines are "really clear." I've been hearing this completely false and disrespectful narrative my entire life.

It's straight up crazy to me that this idea of "crossing over" still persists, as if there's some invisible boundary between Black and white audiences. Damn, what year is this? Are we really supposed to believe that white audiences can't appreciate a Black artist right out the gate, so a Black artist has to win over Black fans first? (Because we all know that's what *urban* means.) Then, once the Black crowd is on board, maybe white folks will give the artist a chance? This idea is offensive in general, and once Frank showed me the charts, I knew it wasn't true.

This is another example of me ignoring the experts and listening to my gut. I didn't care how many music executives told me that I had to start off in R & B. Just because no Black artist had started off and succeeded in pop music, that didn't mean I couldn't. Someone had to be the first, right? So why couldn't it be me?

Frank and I decided that as long as I had good songs, people would respond. If I built it, they would come. And I had no doubt that I could write good songs. I love writing songs in any genre, but I was strategic from the beginning about writing urban music for other artists and pop songs for myself.

Instead of worrying about "crossing over," I looked at the data again to find out what made people tick. I constantly studied the charts to discover what the masses were liking and listening to the most. People tend to put celebrities in one big box and assume that if two artists have roughly the same level of fame, they also have the same level of sales. But fame does not always equal sales or streams. What songs are really *connecting* to the masses?

Most artists just create, hoping they'll reach as many people as possible with the art that is truest to them. I come from a totally different perspective. Yes, everything I create is true to me, but I love all kinds of music. So, choosing what kind of music I would make was a more calculated decision. I wanted to reach as many people as possible and brought the mindset of a record label to my art to make the music that would have the greatest potential reach.

Armed with that data, I've always focused on writing the songs that I thought the highest number of people could relate to and—this part is super important—would want to sing along to. I also make sure to focus on finding a melody that will make people all over the world want to move. This is why I make it a point to infuse my songs and music videos with a diverse range of international vibes and why the melody of a song has always been king to me. If the melody is dope, I know the song is going to be big.

Once I find the melody that speaks to me and really sticks in my head, I put a lyric to it. This is the second biggest piece of the puzzle: writing memorable lines that a vast number of people will want to sing along to, even if English isn't their first language. I always have this in my mind when I'm writing a song. I imagine myself in different scenarios and think about what I would want to say in those moments.

If I was on the dance floor, what would I want to sing to the girl I was dancing with? If I was in the car with my boys, what lyrics would I want to sing along with them? What would I want to say to my girl during sex? Or if I was apologizing to her for something I did, what would I want to say then? What lyrics could I imagine the biggest group of people in a packed stadium singing back to me?

We're all different, and we're all unique, but the truth is that we're also all basically the same when it comes to these moments. They're personal and universal at the same time. As a songwriter, I am essentially people's voice. Not everyone can write songs, so I try to put words to the things that I imagine they'd want to say if they could. It genuinely means a lot to me to be a part of their lives during these small, meaningful moments.

I also want to create something that will move people. Whether it makes them want to cry, dance, or fall in love, it has to evoke a strong emotion. This is why we listen to music. It's the backdrop of our already eventful lives.

Even though I completely trust my gut, I don't just take my own word for it once I decide on a melody or a lyric. As I mentioned earlier, I take a song that I've written and play it for everyone I can. Everyone, that is, who's in my target demo.

Again, it takes research to find out who's in your demo. You need to have the data. Who is your audience? Who do you *want* to be in your audience? Do your research. Find out who else is creating the same type of product as you and who their audience is. How can you capture those eyeballs and then expand on that base audience even more?

To me, it doesn't really matter what anyone outside of my target demo thinks of my music. I mean, I love and respect my mom more than pretty much anyone else, but she was like, "Please do not put out 'Talk Dirty.'" LOL. Sorry, Ma, but I knew that the people in my demo would love that song—and they did.

The thing about focusing on the most popular genre or the most highly valued form of any art is that it's going to be competitive. A bigger potential audience equals more competitors trying to break in. You have to truly be the GOAT to make it to the top of that mountain. But that's okay! You already know that if you focus and put in the work, you can become the best in the world at anything you want to do. And you're going to have a lot of fun along the way.

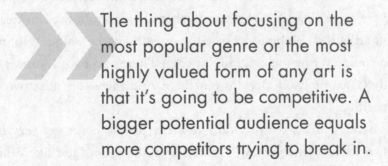

The thing about focusing on the most popular genre or the most highly valued form of any art is that it's going to be competitive. A bigger potential audience equals more competitors trying to break in.

By focusing on the data as much—and sometimes even more than—my art, I was able to do something that no one else has ever done: break out as a Black male pop star without first establishing an urban base. Best of all, I've been able to mix together all the different genres I love to create a pop sound that is completely unique to me.

Even though I'm trying to create music that will appeal to the biggest possible audience, I never want to blend in. I want to stick out like a thumb that's sore as hell. That desire keeps me on my toes, always searching for a new sound that I respond to. I know by now that if something intrigues me, chances are that it will stand out to the rest of the world, too.

See, it's not enough to rely on what's popular in order to succeed; you have to put your own unique spin on it. You want to be mainstream, but you also want to stand out, or else you'll just get lost in the crowd. Art is always a creation from your own perspective. That means it's got to have your personal touch.

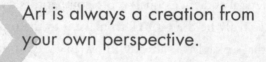

Art is always a creation from your own perspective.

The thing that makes all art so amazing is the fact that every single person is different. That means that no matter how mainstream your art is, if it's going to be true to you, it has to be unique. No one else could ever be me in a million years. There's no two Beyoncés or Lady Gagas or Jason Derulos out there. And there sure ain't two of you, either.

Besides, artists who sound like other people never get very far. When I hear someone say, "Oh my God, she sounds just like Whitney," I'm like, *Okay, she's never making it.* We already have Whitney's music. Audiences want to listen to, watch, or buy things that are different from what they already have. If you were a clothing designer, you wouldn't expect folks to buy two identical items of clothing from different brands, would you? Well, the same thing goes for music and any other art form, too.

Yes, data is king, but it will only get you so far. The final, magical piece of the puzzle is *you*—your spark, your talent, and your unique voice. To find that piece and complete the puzzle, you've got to be bold and try new things. The analytics and the creativity have to go hand in hand. That means you should use the data to guide you, but make sure you don't lose yourself along the way.

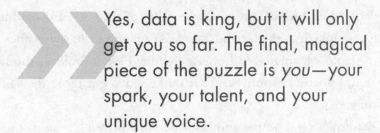

> Yes, data is king, but it will only get you so far. The final, magical piece of the puzzle is *you*—your spark, your talent, and your unique voice.

By the way, everything I just said about music and art also applies to social media, from the importance of data to the magic that only you can bring. Plenty of people out there just post whatever they feel like. Their feed is a random mishmash of their lunch, their kids, and some meme they thought was funny. That's fine, but it's not how you're going to create a brand for yourself online. If that's what you want to do, you have to approach social media as a business just like any other.

When I started getting serious about social media, I took some time to learn about it and study my audience. What were they watching and responding to the most? I used data to find out what was working and what wasn't and analyzed every detail: the number of views, likes, and comments, and exactly which moment during a video people were most likely to click off. I found that about 75 percent of the most successful TikTok videos out there were comedic, so I was like, *Okay, cool, I'll do a bunch of comedic shit, too.*

At that point, I had already gotten rid of the fake sultry artist vibe and started letting my sense of humor loose on TikTok, but I started focusing on this much more. Just as with my music, I always trusted that if I found something funny, my audience would, too.

First, I tried posting a couple of funny sketch videos. I did a series where one of my friends put on a Harry Potter–style invisibility cloak and started messing with me. (We called it an "Invisible Cape"— don't come at me, JK!) In the first video, my friend comes up to me and slaps me in the face out of nowhere, but of course I can't see him, and I'm spooked. In the second, he sneaks up and steals my waffles as I'm trying to eat them, but because he's invisible it looks as though they're just floating in mid-air. That waffle video got more than fifty million views.

Two days later, I posted another video that played like a short film (a very short film). The caption was "Actual footage of me coming out of my cave for a snack." With a blanket as my "cape" and frantic "Flight of the Bumblebee" background music, the video shows me dashing out of my room, down the stairs, and into the kitchen, grabbing all the snacks, and trying to sneak back upstairs.

We utilized different camera angles and individual shots, but what made the video really funny was the reaction shots from my dog, Ice. He wanted those snacks, too. My followers rewarded our production value and Ice's brilliant comedic timing with twenty-five million views.

I was floored. I had never had a run of consecutive eight-figure view counts like that before. It was clear that my fans appreciated my goofy sense of humor—and that they really loved my dog. Who could blame them for either of those things? I got so many comments about Ice that four days later we shot a ridiculous video of him eating a bowl of cereal like a human, with my hands holding the spoon. Another twenty-five million views.

That week alone, I gained more than five million new followers on TikTok. *Five million.* In one week. Let that sink in for a minute. People who knew me only as a singer, or who didn't know me at all, were suddenly laughing along with me. This just goes to show the importance of knowing your target audience.

Once you have the data, it pays to be consistent. The more focused your page is on a specific type of content, voice, or audience you are trying to reach, the easier it will be to know what kind of products you can use it to sell in the future. A lot of successful influencers make the mistake of trying to capitalize on their platform and sell something that's outside of what they're known for. It doesn't always translate.

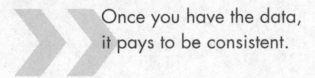

> Once you have the data, it pays to be consistent.

For example, if your audience consistently comes to your page to see fashion, they might not be so interested in buying your music. They're not there to hear you sing. So if you want to sell music, start with music. If you want to sell fashion, start with fashion. The sooner you make these decisions and the more consistent you are, the easier it will be.

Just as I was able to mix genres to create a unique sound, I was able to stay consistent while keeping my online content fresh by creating specific themes that are all united by my own sense of humor and my own unique vibe. I think of my page as a network like HBO, with multiple series that all fit underneath the Jason Derulo umbrella. This way, I appeal to as many people as possible while maintaining some sense of consistency among the social media chaos.

Mainstream success in any medium all comes down to fitting in while standing out at the same time. If you can do that, there's no limit to how far you can go. But you won't be able to get there if you're not armed with data and information. That's like trying to follow a path in the dark. Light up your path with knowledge, and it will light up your future, too.

11

COLLABORATE, PERIOD.

« »

CHOOSE PEOPLE YOU CAN
TEACH *AND* LEARN FROM.

Better yourself each day, little by little,
and you will soon see positive results,
for yourself and for others.

— WILL SMITH

Yes, I may be a control freak and a solo artist, but I still recognize that all art is ultimately a collaboration. Not only that, but all art is better for it.

I often write my songs with co-writers. I often use beats from producers. I love featuring other artists on my songs. And as soon as I get into the studio, I work with producers and sound mixers to create the right sound. To make my music videos, I work with choreographers and dancers and lighting experts and camera technicians. And on social media, I pull in both friends and professionals to help bring my vision to life. Hell, even this book was a collaboration between quite a few people who helped make it a reality. When it comes to creating, no one is an island, nor should they be.

No matter who is collaborating with you, the best collaborations don't just help you execute your ideas. They allow you to mix completely different worlds together to create something new. This means collaborating with people outside your genre and sometimes even outside your industry. Some of my most successful (and fun) collaborations have been completely out of the box, unpredictable, and just plain weird. I wouldn't have it any other way.

Back in 2014, I was coming off the success of the *Talk Dirty* album, which I had written while I was recovering from my neck injury. Because I had wanted to create something that people could really move to, that album included a lot of up-tempo club songs and incorporated more hip-hop and R & B sounds than my first two.

On *Talk Dirty*, I was able to collaborate with some great artists. I featured Snoop Dogg, who is one of the coolest people around, on the song "Wiggle." I love the fact that Snoop is just down for whatever, and he has absolutely no ego. With Snoop, the guy you see on TV is the same guy you meet in person. He's always just Snoop, and it was a lot of fun working with him. On that album, I also featured Tyga on the song "Bubblegum" and Kid Ink on "Kama Sutra." Their features were lit, and each of these artists added value to the songs, but none of them was exactly unexpected.

Now, it was time to change all that.

People are often surprised to hear that I love country music. As

I said earlier, I love music in general. That love isn't limited to one specific genre, and I've never wanted to restrain myself to one genre, either, even though I chose to focus on pop music. In particular, I love the songwriting in country music. It's real songwriter's music, so it's always dope for me to listen to.

I wanted to share this other musical side of myself with my fans, but I knew that it would be too much of a departure for me to suddenly release a country song or a whole album of country songs. You've got to keep evolving, but it's also important to maintain some consistency so people know who you are and what you're about.

So when the opportunity came my way, I jumped at the chance to collaborate with country stars and dip my toe into their world. In 2014, I got a call from Florida Georgia Line (FGL), a country duo whose debut single had broken sales records. They wanted me to get on a remix of their song "This Is How We Roll," which was also going to feature Luke Bryan.

It sounded like a hit to me. I appreciated the fact that FGL wanted to extend the life of the song by making it appeal more to a pop audience, and I thought it was a great idea for me to be introduced to a new audience, as well. I also knew that the collaboration would surprise my fans and that it might be shocking to country music fans. But to me, it's value added when I can work with artists who have a completely different fan base from mine. I see it as a way of inviting more people to join the party. How can that be a bad thing?

I also believe that all of the barriers we put up between genres are so easily broken. We humans created those categories to define and sell records. Music doesn't naturally divide itself up like that, and people don't really care what genre a song is in as long as that song touches them. In fact, music is often better when those lines are blurred or erased completely.

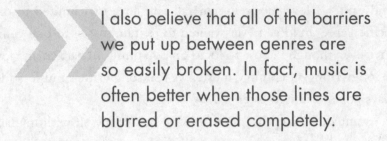

I also believe that all of the barriers
we put up between genres are
so easily broken. In fact, music is
often better when those lines are
blurred or erased completely.

However, I also know that the country audience is very passion-ate about their music. I wasn't sure how they'd react to an outsider like me inserting myself into their world. I was too excited to worry about that, though. I had fun writing my verse on "This Is How We Roll" and loved going into the studio and recording something com-pletely different. It was like working a muscle I'd never used before at the gym.

Once the song was released and started to do its thing, FGL asked me to perform with them at the Country Music Association (CMA) Awards. Even better, I would be opening the show with FGL, Luke Bryan, and ZZ Top, doing a mash-up of our songs, including "This Is How We Roll" and "Talk Dirty." Yo, a great artist is a great artist, and I was honored to be on the stage with those guys.

I met Luke and the guys behind FGL for the first time when we were rehearsing for the show. You might be surprised to hear me say this, but I hit it off with them more than with almost any other artists I've met. They were real human beings, normal down-to-earth guys like myself. I was also impressed by how amped they were to dance with me during the show. They really wanted to go for it, and I always appreciate that mindset in another artist.

As soon as we hit the stage, the entire crowd went nuts. They loved it, and it was so much fun to see the other guys let loose on "Talk Dirty." At that point, I considered myself to be right: music is music, and it transcends artificial barriers. If a song moves people, then that's really all that matters. The guys I was performing with that night certainly felt that way, and the audience did, too.

I was shocked after the show when I started receiving more racist comments than I've ever gotten in my entire life. Of course, I've always known that racism is alive and well. I've faced it a time or two, no doubt. But I had never experienced anything like this: comment after comment saying things like "Stay away from our music!" (That was actually one of the nicer comments.)

It was a lot, but my main reaction was to feel bad for these people. To be so small-minded and ignorant is a really sad place to be. It's miserable to carry around so much hate. And although it was hurtful to be on the receiving end of those comments, I knew that in the big picture, their racism hurt them more than it hurt me.

Plus, these folks were hiding behind a screen. The audience that had actually seen me perform had loved it. That's what really mattered.

By then, I had started to build a relationship with Luke and the guys from FGL. One day, Luke called me up and said, "Hey, Jason, you should come by and stay at my place." (Imagine the accent as you're reading this.) "You can stay at my barn."

"Yo, enough with the racist stuff," I told him. "I'm not staying in your barn."

Luke just laughed. "It's not what you think," he told me.

Of course, when I showed up, I discovered that his barn was super plush. But it was still country through and through. I had on my chains, some big diamonds in my ears, ripped jeans that were a little tighter than they used to be, and a dope pair of high-tops. Luke took one look at me and handed me some boots, a button-up flannel shirt, and a pair of wide-legged jeans.

I was completely out of my element but completely in my element at the same time. While I've always been a city boy—going from Miami to New York to LA—it felt great to slow the pace down for a minute. We spent the whole weekend shooting discs, drinking beer, singing a little, and just hanging out. I had the time of my life.

Luke and the guys from FGL and I continued to make music together, for no other reason than it's what we love to do and we had fun doing it together. A few years later, FGL and I collaborated on another song called "Women" that they released, which was an all-encompassing celebration and really magical, in my opinion.

Luke and I have also continued our friendship and have collaborated many times since then. We did an episode of Country Music Television's *Crossroads*—he sang six of my songs and I sang six of his. It was a huge hit, and I had so much fun onstage with Luke, especially watching him sing his heart out to songs like "Talk Dirty." My boy killed it!

Now that the country music community had (mostly) embraced me, I decided it was time for my audience to start hearing a little country, too. I was already working on the song "Broke" when Barack Obama, who was president at the time, invited me to a dinner at the White House. Keith Urban had already agreed to play banjo on the track, and I was planning to have some harmonica on it, as well. So when I got to the White House all done up in my tux and saw that I was sitting near Stevie Wonder, I almost lost my mind.

Back up for a second. I had been a huge fan of Stevie's for years. I remember going to the record store as a kid and buying my first box set of his albums. For those of you who are too young to know, a box set is a group of an artist's albums bundled together as a set. Stevie and I got to talking, and the whole time, I was thinking about how crazy it would be if I could get Stevie to play harmonica on "Broke."

I didn't know what Stevie would say, but I did know that if I didn't ask, it definitely wouldn't happen. I had to shoot my shot.

"Stevie," I finally asked, "would you like to play harmonica on one of my songs?"

Right away, Stevie was like, "Of course, man, we're family." I was hyped, and I thought, *This is going well—maybe I can push a little more.*

"Would you like to sing on the song, too?"

Stevie said, "Put it like this. If I hear the song on the radio and I'm not on it, I'm gonna whoop your ass."

With "Broke," my fan base embraced that country sound just as much as the country music crowd had embraced me. I gained a whole new audience and a lot of credibility as a versatile artist who can work in different genres and blend them together to create something new. It was also such an incredible feeling to have one of my heroes be a part of what I created. Working with Stevie was nothing short of amazing.

One thing I've found while collaborating is that, most of the time, the artists at the highest levels have no ego. They have nothing to prove. They're just locked into doing their thang. It's the ones who feel like they have to prove themselves who put up a façade, and that's never a good look for anyone.

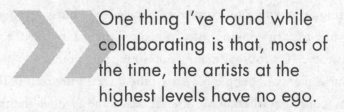

> One thing I've found while collaborating is that, most of the time, the artists at the highest levels have no ego.

But as much as I've loved collaborating with some of the biggest and best artists out there, I've found that some of the most impactful collaborations of my career have been with my own followers and fans.

You may have never considered the idea of collaborating with your heroes *or* your fans, and I'm not saying you should cold-call Stevie

Wonder. But the fastest way to pop on any social media network is to grab the attention of other creators on the platform. Once you have been blessed by the best, their masses will migrate to your content.

On Instagram and Facebook, collaborating usually just means that another creator shares your work with their followers. That's great and all, but it's not nearly as impactful as a true collaboration, which is much easier to pull off on TikTok. This is one of the reasons I love the app so much. You can create whatever you want with anyone you want, even if you've never met or spoken to them.

The best way to grab the attention of TikTok royalty is by adding value to their content with a "duet." The duet feature allows you to appear side by side in a split screen with any video on the platform and interact indirectly with your favorite creators. You can sing or play a duet with musicians, salivate over a chef's delicious recipes, or even laugh at or improve on a comedian's joke while filming your reaction in real time.

Keep in mind that every time the biggest TikTok creators post a video, hundreds or thousands of people will "duet" the content. If you want your collaboration to cut through the noise and grab your target's attention, your duet needs to be transformative. This is your chance to do something surprising. Don't just add a new video—add a new *genre*. Use your duet to turn cooking into comedy, sexiness into science, or pets into parodies. Or, for that matter, pop music into country.

Of course, plenty of people have used the duet feature on TikTok to duet my content. Others have directly asked me to duet theirs. I love doing this to highlight other creators with content that I enjoy, especially when it leads to a transformative or surprising duet.

In 2020, when my TikTok was really getting hot, a user named Dalton (@daltontherockjohnson) posted a video of himself singing "In My Head." He opened the video by saying, "Hey, if you're Jason Derulo, duet this. You're gonna sing the blue line, ok?"

This video got my attention for a few reasons. First of all, Dalton and I could not have appeared to be more different. He was a big, middle-aged white guy in shorts, a baggy T-shirt, and sandals, standing in what looked like a very Midwestern yard. But he actually had a good singing voice and was totally unselfconscious as he let loose with some pretty sweet and hilarious dance moves. His whole video was a great example of the saying "You can't judge a book by its cover."

But the funniest part of the video was the fact that the only lyric that was written in blue (meaning it was a line that I was supposed to sing), was the opening of the song: "Jason Derulo." Dalton literally just wanted me to sing my name.

This was so hilarious to me, because most singing duets that use colored lines like this involve harmonies or alternating lyrics between the two people in the video, especially when the duet is with a celebrity. But Dalton didn't want me to harmonize or sing back and forth with him. He just wanted to use my patented intro as a funny setup for him to sing his version of the song.

By making me laugh, Dalton nailed the duet invitation. I loved the fact that he had the guts to just go for it, and of course I went ahead and accepted. In the duet, I sang my name out loud, and then danced along on my side of the screen as Dalton sang his heart out to "In My Head." I wasn't surprised to see that my followers loved the video—and Dalton himself—just as much as I did.

Since then, I've been using my platform more and more to highlight up-and-coming creators. I love to reach out to people who I think can make it but need a real shot, and discovering new talent has become one of my favorite things to do. I never forget the fact that I used to be that person who wanted an opportunity so badly, and it felt as if it took forever for anyone to really listen to me. It's amazing to now be in the position to give others a stage for their content, both online and off.

Whether they're a huge star or a complete unknown, everyone that I decide to collaborate with is someone I'm already a fan of in some way. I trust that if I find a person compelling, my audience will, too. I'm more than happy for these creators to utilize me as a gateway to their success, and I don't need anything back. It's not that kind of vibe. I *want* to be a springboard for them.

I do the same thing when it comes to music. People come up to me all the time and tell me they make music. No matter who they are, I always ask them to email me their stuff, and I always listen to it. Sure, I'm helping them out, but truthfully, this helps me, as well. You just never know where the next big talent is going to come from. Most artists who stand the test of time surround themselves with others who are still innovating, and I'm no different.

There's so little that's new under the sun. So how do you continue to grow and change and keep people guessing? I've been able to do this by finding inspiration from other people who have a new sound of their own.

The only way to have a lasting career is to stay on that cutting edge. You have to take any and all opportunities, no matter where they come from. I may have great ideas, but other people do, too, and I want all them ideas on the table—the ones I come up with, the ones from the guys and girls who are popping, and the ones from the guys and girls who are just starting out.

The only way to have a lasting career is to stay on that cutting edge. You have to take any and all opportunities, no matter where they come from.

So, on your way up, don't forget to reach back out and help someone along the way. It'll be rewarding from a humanistic standpoint and could help drive your ship closer to the promised land. Giving back is the gift that keeps on giving. There's nothing like the feeling that comes from seeing someone you helped become a success story. And a lot of times that person will also come back and help you in some way.

Don't worry for one second about giving a boost to someone who may end up being your competition in the future. I truly believe that there is room in this world for everyone to succeed. Also, it's a joke to worry about competing against one person when you should be worried about competing against Hulu and Amazon Prime and Snapchat. There are so many different things grabbing people's attention nowadays. One other person can't make a dent in your success in the grand scheme of things.

The only person you should always compete against is you—to become the best version of yourself that you can be. I spend every day thinking about how I can best myself. Right now, for me, this means becoming a leader. When people first started calling me the "King of TikTok," it felt like a lot of pressure. I wasn't sure that I was worthy of that title. But I decided to embrace it and lead from a place of love and positivity, and the results—both for me and others—have been incredible.

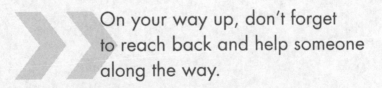

> On your way up, don't forget to reach back and help someone along the way.

Whatever you do, wear that crown with pride and become the king or queen that you were meant to be. Help others, draw from others, and open yourself up to finding collaborators in unexpected places. When you stop seeing other people as competition and instead start seeing them as people who can either learn something from you or teach you something—or both—a whole new world of success and inspiration will open up for you.

12

REVEAL YOURSELF IN YOUR BEST LIGHT.

« »

IGNORE WHAT WORKS FOR EVERYONE ELSE.

One of the first music videos I directed was for the song, "If It Ain't Love." It's a sexy song and an even sexier video that features me with an incredible female dancer in an office setting. The moves are hot, and we added in some fun acrobatics. I'm in a three-piece suit, she's in a secretary-style shirt with a bun in her hair that's straight out of a fantasy, and we're literally dancing on the ceiling. It's pretty dope.

Of course, I put my heart and countless hours into every detail of that video. But when I look at it now, I cringe. I still love the concept and the choreography, but to me, the video looks lackluster. And honestly, I'm not surprised.

The entire time we were shooting that video, I was worried that the lighting wasn't right. As the director, I was constantly going back and forth from in front of the camera to the screen to look at what we had just shot. And every time I checked, I wasn't happy.

"It looks dull," I said to the director of photography (DP), who's in charge of the lighting. I had been saying this all day.

"Trust me," he said for what felt like the five-billionth time. "I'll lighten it in postproduction. We'll make it super colorful and vibrant. You'll see."

Seriously, if I had a penny for every time a DP said something similar to me . . . well, I don't need them pennies. But you get the point. Even before I started directing my own videos, I was constantly fighting with DPs about lighting. They think they know best because they're experts and they've lit some of the biggest people in the world. That's cool—but it doesn't mean they know how to light *me*.

Once again, here was an expert telling me that he knew me better than me. And once again, he was wrong. No surprise, when we sat down to edit the video together, I thought it looked dark and flat. "Make it brighter," I said over and over, and he did his best, but it was too late to fix the fundamental issue and make it as vibrant as I wanted.

Despite what DPs are always telling me, there's only so much you can do in post, and I was really disappointed. The song did okay, but it wasn't a huge hit. I believe if that video had been lit the way I wanted from the beginning, it would have taken the song to a different level.

The next year, I directed the video for "Tip Toe." I was inspired by what Missy Elliot had done in her time and wanted to make a video that wasn't as conceptual as "If It Ain't Love," but that invited the audience to travel to different worlds with me in a series of vignettes. At the same time, I wanted it to be bright and fun and very dance-centric.

This wasn't just what *I* wanted. I was constantly studying my audience and what they responded to. With all of my videos, I scoured the number of YouTube views and likes and comments. *What are they liking? What are the comments saying? What is getting the highest number of views?*

You can learn a lot from the internet if you're strong enough to look through the BS, and I learned that my particular audience wanted a lot of dancing, a lot of bright colors, and a lot of fun. Today, I'm one of the most viewed musicians on YouTube *ever*, and that's because I've always tried to give my fans what they want instead of following the trends or listening to anyone who tried to convince me to do something different.

For "Tip Toe," I decided to create a jungle and have some amazing dancers become a part of it, and also take viewers to Japan and to a golden kingdom that felt almost biblical. Most of the preproduction process was similar to my other videos. Even when I'm not directing, I'm always there for the casting, choosing every model and dancer. I decide on the costumes, and I work hand in hand with the choreographers.

This time, though, shooting the video was different, namely because I was a complete stickler for the lighting. I had learned my lesson the last time. After every single shot, I checked the screen, and if I wasn't happy with the lighting, we would not move on until we got it right. No more nonsense about fixing it in post.

Another huge surprise—that video came out exactly how I'd imagined it. It's not one of my most viewed videos at two hundred million views, but that's still a hell of a lot more than "If It Ain't Love." The song itself was more successful, too.

« »

With music videos and on social media, it's just as much of an art as it is a science to get people to stop scrolling and keep their eyeballs on you. In some ways, this is even harder to do on social media. Today, there's more noise on social media than literally anywhere else. The idea of finding a way to cut through all that noise may seem daunting, or even impossible.

Social media matters because it is where the eyeballs are. Having someone's attention, even for a short period of time, is the most valuable commodity in the world. How are you going to know what is special about your art (or what sucks about it!) if you don't give people a chance to see it?

You may be convinced of the idea that you need to be precious and humble about your craft, sweating in the shadows before you can emerge as a genius or prodigy ready to claim all of the trophies waiting for you. Stop believing that lie. You need motivation to get better. No matter what you want to accomplish in this life, getting more eyeballs on you gives you a higher platform to stand on. It gives you more information and more confidence, and you'll need both to reach your dreams. Trust me.

To this day, I fall victim to overthinking my posts on social media. When I first started posting on TikTok, I was creatively carefree and at my most mentally healthy place in terms of my relationship with social media. I was posting one video after the other, and my mind was in the zone. This gave me a healthy detachment from each video's success. If one didn't hit, it was just a temporary thing, and I was already on to the next as part of my routine.

Fast forward three years, and now I'm not as creatively carefree on social media. The less often I post, the more concerned I am with each video's reception. I don't have the same routine of posting one video after the other, and that's when a less healthy relationship with social media starts to emerge.

I'm glad I'm writing this down for me to read back later. I know what I have to do, and you probably do, too, but we have to constantly remind ourselves. This book will be my reminder. Let it be yours, too. The titles of each chapter will help you remember to stay on course on your journey to greatness.

>> I know what I have to do, and you probably do, too, but we have to constantly remind ourselves. This book will be my reminder. Let it be yours, too.

Posting on social media is a nonnegotiable, but it shouldn't be a chore. To succeed, you have to start looking at it as a creative outlet and an opportunity. You can get more eyeballs on your work through social media than literally anywhere else, and the world is moving more in that direction every single day. It is a great equalizer and feedback machine. Essentially obliterating the barriers to entry for every kind of artistic or creative pursuit, social media has made this era the age of artists, and it is only getting better.

One of the reasons that I love social media and that it works so well for aspiring creatives is that it celebrates the individual. Audiences flock to social media platforms to experience something new, different, and authentic. Now, you can capture the world's attention just by doing what you do, just by being you.

Alright, if you're rolling your eyes, I get it. I know it isn't as easy as hitting "post." And here's why . . . You ready? Count with me. One, two . . . Okay, stop, that's it. That's the amount of time you have to grab someone's attention. And that tiny amount of time is only shrinking.

People used to say that humans had an eight-second attention span. But today that's a joke. Having a full eight seconds to get someone's attention would be a huge luxury in the world we're living in today.

One of the reasons social media is a great tool for creators is that it teaches us the lesson I learned back at that audition—not to waste a moment, to make every second count and matter, to get to the point faster. It is a training ground for what works and what doesn't. With so much noise out there, if you want people to focus on you, you've really got to go out of your way to grab their attention right out the gate.

Just think about how fast you scroll through your social media feed and how distracted you are when you're doing it. While you're scrolling, you're also waiting in line at the store or running on the treadmill. It's the exact same situation when you're streaming music or even when you're scrolling around on Netflix, trying to decide what to watch.

Half the time, you're not even paying attention to what songs and images and videos and TV shows you're racing right past. You might be missing out on something amazing, but you'll never know it. Your brain is just subconsciously waiting for something to come along and grab you, forcing you to stop in your tracks.

So how are you going to get these eyeballs on you and keep them there for as long as possible? At the end of the day, it's all about you saying to the world, "I have something for you."

As consumers, we're all selfish, and we all have our own needs. We're going to give our attention to someone only if we believe there's something in it for us—some sort of value. This value might come in the form of information, knowledge, a laugh, or simply a feeling, even if it lasts for only a short amount of time.

It's helpful to think of the social media relationship as primarily transactional. No one is going to watch you or listen to your content just because you seem to be a nice person or because you mean well. Being good-looking may help a little, sure, but you still have to provide viewers with some sort of value beyond just a pretty face.

The first thing I do before I write a song, post a video on TikTok, or share any type of content is to figure out exactly what I'm trying to give to my audience and what value they are going to get in exchange for their time.

For me, it almost always comes down to making people *feel* something. Holistically speaking, I want everything that I create to provide people with a small piece of happiness. This may be in the form of a quick burst of energy while they're getting ready in the morning, a few minutes of fun while they're dancing at the club, or a moment to chill and breathe during a difficult day. I'm not a superemotional guy, so it's kind of ironic that my goal is to create emotions in others, but that's truly what brings me fulfillment, especially when it allows me to become a part of people's everyday lives.

I also know that this is the value that my audience wants to get from my particular content. We all want to feel something. We want to laugh, we want to cry, we want to dance, we want to fall in love, and we want to be independent when we've fallen out of love. Since long before social media ever existed, we've relied on creators to help us get through these moments.

 We want to laugh, we want to cry, we want to dance, we want to fall in love, and we want to be independent when we've fallen out of love. Since long before social media ever existed, we've relied on creators to help us get through these moments.

But my audience won't have a chance to feel anything if they don't stop and listen to my music or watch my videos. A lot more people got something out of "Tip Toe" than they did from "If It Ain't Love," only because the vibrancy of the video caught their attention.

Of course, once I started getting serious about social media, I brought my obsession with lighting with me, using what I'd learned along the way to make compelling content. This is one of my secret weapons, but it's just as important for anyone who wants eyeballs on them.

I can tell you with certainty that the number one most important thing that you can do to make your posts stand out is to get your lighting right. This goes for any type of visual content and even video calls. In fact, all of my tips for shooting video content can also make you look better in that next Zoom meeting or interview.

When it comes to social media, lighting can be the deciding factor that determines whether someone is going to scroll right by your video or stop and watch it. Viewers simply will not watch your video if they can't see you or what's happening clearly.

Good lighting tells your viewers, "This video is worth watching." Going the extra mile here can take your visual content from good to great. I don't care if you're dancing, filming DIY projects, cooking, or doing comedy. Don't turn that camera on until you've figured out your lighting. It's honestly that important.

The idea of creating a whole lighting setup may seem overwhelming, but there are ways to do this that are simple and affordable. The three most important things for you to think about when lighting your videos are making sure that you have enough light, making sure that your light is even, and making sure that your light is coming from the right direction.

A camera lens needs way more light than the human eye to create an image that looks good. But if that light is uneven, it will cast ugly shadows on your face. And if it's coming from the wrong direction, it can lead to a harsh glare that will make people click off your video faster than almost anything else.

To make sure that you have enough light, start by taking advantage of natural sunlight. There is really no light in the world you can purchase that is better than the sun, and best of all, that shit is free. Make sure to shoot your videos in a room that gets plenty of natural sunlight or, even better, shoot them outside.

If you're inside, position yourself so there's a window behind the camera and the sun is shining directly on your face. Never shoot with the window behind you or whoever is the subject of your video. If you can shoot outside, the best time of day to film your video is either during the half hour right after the sun rises in the morning or within the hour right before the sun sets at night. This is when the light is the softest, the most flattering, and the least likely to create those ugly shadows. It's called "the magic hour" for a reason, even though it's technically an hour and a half.

If natural sunlight is unavailable to you and you have even a modest budget for lighting, buying some simple lights is a great investment that will dramatically enhance your videos. Even a small ring light will make a big difference. You can also utilize the lighting that you already have. When shooting at night, place a lamp on either side of your face to light yourself evenly. Just make sure to use the same types of bulbs in each lamp so you don't have two different light sources competing with each other.

Even with great lighting, one thing that most people overlook is learning how to properly light themselves personally, not just their videos in general. You can have a great setup, but if it doesn't complement your own particular skin color and features, it's useless. It doesn't matter what works for the rest of the world. You have to figure out what works best for you. This goes for everything, not just your lighting, but we'll stick to this subject just for the moment.

There's no one lighting setup that works for everyone. Darker skin is less reflective than lighter skin, so if you have darker skin as I do, it's even more important to make sure you have adequate lighting. Whatever your skin color is, start by finding a photo of yourself that you like. Then try to replicate the lighting in the picture as you are positioning different lights.

Once you have enough lighting, you've got to make sure that it's even to avoid creating shadows. Try diffusing the light with some kind of filter. Otherwise, bright lights can look really harsh and un-flattering on camera. Of course, there are tons of lighting filters out there that you can buy, and many of them are inexpensive. You can also use household objects like window curtains or even a shower curtain to soften your lights. Experiment with different things to see what looks best on *you*.

Finally, make sure that your lights are in the right place. Normally, you want your lights to be at about the same height as your face, but sometimes this can create a glare. To avoid this, raise the lights higher and move them further away from you. Avoiding glare is especially important if you wear glasses or have any other reflective objects within the frame of your video.

Once you have your lighting basics in place, you can add a few extras to make your videos pop. To get viewers' attention and keep them watching the whole video instead of moving on halfway through, I like to utilize bursts of color throughout the video that add incredible texture and grab people's attention just when it might be starting to slip. By adding something unexpected like this, I'm making sure that viewers never have a chance to get bored.

To accomplish this, I bought some inexpensive lights that can change color in the middle of a video. These are especially fun to use in videos where I'm dancing. This little trick is so subtle that viewers don't even really notice it or realize why they're so drawn to the video. They just know that they're really enjoying it, and it's all because of creative lighting that serves as irresistible eye candy.

Speaking of colors, try to avoid wearing white or black in your videos. Besides the fact that a pop of color in your wardrobe is more likely to grab viewers' attention, extreme colors like those are difficult to properly light. Similarly, try to avoid shooting your videos against plain white walls. They're boring, and they can cause the light to bounce all over the place.

Take the time to think about your background. If you're shooting at home, do you have a room with a gallery wall, some funky wallpaper, or a bookcase that can add color and texture to your video? If all else fails, at least try to find a background with a more interesting color than plain old white.

Outside of lighting, I utilize a few different tricks that you can easily replicate to grab people's attention in your videos. Over the years, I noticed that my music videos were more successful if they included some close-ups of my face. People watching your video want to feel you and get a sense of who you are, so close-ups are super important, especially in the early part of a video.

A lot of times, I start my videos with an extreme close-up to quickly grab viewers' attention. This is like me shouting, "Here I am!" It stops viewers in their tracks before they even have a chance to scroll by. Then I back off. Sometimes I switch it up and open the video with a plain background and then quickly pop into the frame for an added element of surprise.

I also always focus on color, taking another cue from my music videos. My brightest and most colorful videos—"Swalla," "Get Ugly," "Tip Toe," and "Wiggle"—together have literally *billions* of views, and I brought what I learned from them with me straight to TikTok.

The biggest lessons that have paid off the most came from my experience creating the video for "Swalla." In fact, this is when it all came together for me.

Instead of directing this video, I chose to work with Gil Green, a great director that both Nicki Minaj and I had worked with in the past. Nicki was all-around incredible to work with. I intentionally choose not to direct videos that feature another artist to avoid any possible awkwardness or creating some sort of hierarchy. I always want it to feel like a fun, natural collaboration, which "Swalla" definitely was.

That said, I was still as involved as ever in creating the video. Gil came to me with the idea to use all different flavors of drinks as the backdrop, but I thought this was too on the nose. Instead, we decided to create "Derulo lollipops" and other candies that would add a lot of color and visual appeal.

Beyond the candy, we went nuts with the colors in that video, from the neon backgrounds to the body paint that was so beautiful, like an art piece. We also added a ton of eye candy (get it?) through the choreography, the water that we danced in (which was cold as hell, by the way), and the all-female band. By then, I knew exactly what my audience wanted, and this was it. On YouTube alone, that video now has two *billion* views.

The other interesting thing about "Swalla" is that the radio stations all said (understandably) that it was too raunchy for them. It got zero radio play. When I released "In My Head" less than a decade before, not getting support from radio stations would have killed the song. A single simply could not become a hit without radio play. It was so important that we rushed back into the studio to rerecord it with new lyrics at the very last minute.

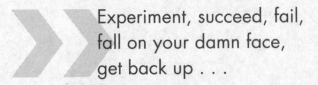

Experiment, succeed, fail, fall on your damn face, get back up . . .

But "Swalla" became one of my biggest hits without any support from radio. I'm talking about billions of streams. This opened my eyes to the fact that we were now living in a very different world than when I started out, with brand-new rules. Now, if people like a song, it's going to be a hit. Period. The barriers for entry are gone. And one of the main factors that made that song a hit was a video that showed me in my best light.

Look, this chapter is all about lighting. Use the techniques I shared, but you don't have to take it all literally. My point is more about figuring out what works for you in every aspect of your work and sharing *that* with the world. Who cares what works for anyone else?

You want to show off *your* best features, *your* biggest talents, and the things that make *you* special. Those are the things that will set you apart from the crowd. Do you even know what they are? Experiment, succeed, fail, fall on your damn face, get back up . . . and who knows? Maybe that video of you falling on your face will be the one that ends up cutting through.

13

TALENT IS
OVERRATED.

《 》

DESIRE IS THE GIFT.

It's imperative to have a team and friends around
that can be truthful and continually help us be
our best selves in all aspects of life.

**—TYLER HUBBARD AND BRIAN KELLEY,
FLORIDA GEORGIA LINE**

I'm not just trying to be modest when I say that I wasn't born with
a lot of talent. And it doesn't really matter how much or how little
talent you were born with, either. The truth is that I started out with
a strong gift for songwriting and maybe a slightly better than average singing voice—just slightly. But as I said, I took what I was born
with and strengthened it over time. I sang more, so I sang better. It's

as simple as that, and it's really just as simple for any talent or skill or knowledge that you're trying to develop, too.

Think about it. How many talented people do you know who never made it anywhere, not even off their damn couch? And how many talented artists do succeed but are here today and gone tomorrow because their work ethic starts to slip once they start to think they've made it? That's because talent isn't everything, and it's not the most important thing. It's just not.

Hearing this may knock some wind out of your sails if you've been sitting back and counting on your alleged gifts to help you succeed. If you're really naturally talented, then you're starting off ahead of the pack. Yo, congrats, but that's nothing to rely on. The people starting the race behind you can catch up and even pass you if they work hard enough and you don't pick up speed.

On the other hand, if you feel like your skills aren't where they need to be right now, I hope it's empowering to consider the idea that talent is overrated. Believing that you're stuck with whatever talents you were born with is just as crazy as thinking that talent is all you need to succeed. Anyone can climb to the top of the mountain if they're willing to put in the work, and that includes you.

No matter where you're starting off, you can get better at anything as long as you practice it. And if you practice it enough, you can become great. I'm not saying it's an even playing field. If you're starting off with less talent and less access than the next person, yeah, it might be a little bit harder for you. It will probably take you a little bit longer to get there. But if you put in the work and stick with it, you can always catch up. This goes for anyone who's trying to make it in any field.

If you want proof, just look at an athlete like LeBron James, who was born ahead of the pack. He is a specimen of a different breed, who clearly has a physical edge on other players. His body is like a cheat code. But then again, there are other guys who also have that kind of advantage and aren't nearly as good as him. Why not? Because they didn't put in the work, plain and simple.

On the flip side, there's Michael Jordan, who didn't start off with nearly the same level of natural talent as LeBron. Jordan didn't even make his high school's varsity basketball team. But he went on to put in the necessary work to become the best in the world.

My point is that in almost every case, there's no such thing as a big enough edge to separate you from someone who is willing to do whatever it takes to catch up. You've got to keep moving forward at the same speed—or faster—if you want to stay ahead. And if you're the one who's behind right now, you are not stuck there.

Michael Jordan may not have been born with the skills, but he was born with the *desire*. And that, y'all, is the real gift—a desire to succeed that is so strong and so intense that it becomes an obsession. There will always be some anomalies, but most of the time, it's not the most talented people who reach the highest levels of success. It's the people with the greatest desire and the biggest obsession.

This desire is exactly the same gift that I was born with, too. I've been straight up obsessed with becoming one of the greatest entertainers in the world ever since I saw Michael Jackson onstage when I was four years old. And I have sacrificed the majority of my life to fulfill that dream.

Maybe my intense work ethic is a genetic gift. If not, I still come by it honestly. As a kid, I learned what hard work really meant from my parents. They were immigrants who worked their butts off to make it in this country. My mom worked two jobs while going to law school. One of those jobs was as an immigration officer. Then she came home and cooked delicious food and made all us kids feel like we were rich, even though we really had next to nothing. Meanwhile, my dad worked around the clock to start his own small import and export business.

Working all the time always seemed normal to me because I saw my parents doing it every day. I didn't know anything different. And I'm so grateful to my parents for modeling that level of discipline.

By the time I was in college at AMDA in New York City, I had one foot planted in the music business, writing songs for other artists. Between that work and my school curriculum and my auditions, I was grinding around the clock. I thought I already knew how to work hard on my own, but that was nothing compared to the workload at AMDA.

I loved it, though. The amount of work that they piled on top of me was invaluable, because it taught me how to juggle and work harder than I ever thought was possible. For the two years I was at AMDA, I had absolutely zero time for anything except my craft. Instead of a burden, I saw this as a huge luxury, and I was determined to make the most of it.

The students I studied with at AMDA were some of the best in the world. It's one of the top schools in America for the arts, and they've got countless alums on Broadway, in movies and TV shows, and in the music industry. When I was there, a lot of the other students were itching to start their careers. I was, too. But the big difference between me and those folks was that some of them complained about being in school, while I was grateful for every minute I was there. "This is a waste of time," they whined. "I just want to get out there and start auditioning and start my career."

Honestly, I didn't understand this mindset at all. How in the world could it be a waste to spend your time improving your craft? Time is only wasted if you're not using it to get better, or if you're half-assing it during the hours of work that you do put in.

See, it's not just about the number of hours that you dedicate to something. It's about putting your all into those hours. It's a cliché for a reason: you get out of something exactly what you put into it.

It's just math, y'all. We all have the same number of hours in the day. If you and me both work at something for an hour, but I put 100 percent of my heart and mind and focus into that hour and you only put in 50 percent, who do you think is going to improve more quickly? And who exactly wasted their time in that equation? I'll tell you one thing: it ain't me.

Here's another way to think about it: when I take a boxing class, I can either really go for it and punch the bag with all my might, or I can just . . . punch the bag halfway. Imagine for a minute that your life is that punching bag. How hard are you going to punch that thing?

If you're happy coasting, there's nothing wrong with putting in 50 percent. Most people go with the flow and let life happen to them. That's okay. I know plenty of people with an average, normal life who are content with that. If that's you, then I'm happy for you. Honestly.

But if you have huge goals and aspirations like I do, know that you'll only reach them if you punch that shit with all your might. Halfway is simply not enough. There are too many other people out there trying to get to the same pot of gold that you are.

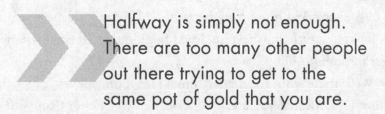

Halfway is simply not enough. There are too many other people out there trying to get to the same pot of gold that you are.

Let me give you an example. A few years ago, a friend of mine I do business with came to me and said that his son does music production and asked me to listen to some of his stuff. I said yes, and his son sent a few beats my way. There's no nicer way to say this: they weren't good.

I knew that I wouldn't be doing this kid any favors if I kept my opinion to myself, so I gave it to him straight. "Go back, lock yourself in a room, and come back to me when you've grown," I told him. "You're not ready yet."

Only ten days later, this dude sent me another set of beats.

I was actually offended. I'm a busy guy. If I'm doing you a favor by listening to your stuff, then you'd better make sure it's tip-top before taking up my time—twice. Did this guy really believe that he could become a great producer in a week and a half?

"These are really, really bad," I told him. "You've gotten no better, and I would be lying if I said I was surprised. A week is not going to get you where you need to be, and the fact that you think you can get there that quickly is crazy to me."

I broke down for him exactly how slim the chances were of his making it in this business, even if he had a connection to someone like me. That wouldn't do him any good if he wasted that shot by shooting it before he was ready. Then I told him about a producer that I signed to my publishing company named Smash David. Besides me, he's worked with Khalid, Chris Brown, Lil Wayne, Big Sean, and some other huge artists. When I met Smash, he was doing seven beats a day, and he was already well established in the business.

I asked this kid how many beats he did a day. "Maybe one," he said, looking a little bit sheepish. I was hoping that I'd finally started to get through to him.

"Well, there you go," I told him. "He's doing seven times the amount of work that you are. Of course, he's way better than you."

Listen to me, and listen good. Amazing doesn't happen overnight. Looking back, this is probably why none of my so-called big breaks turned out to be breaks at all. At the time, I thought I was ready, but I wasn't. I wasn't there yet. When I was a kid winning singing competitions all over Florida, I was good, but I wasn't great. By the time

I'd made it onstage at the Apollo, I was great, but I wasn't undeniable. At least, not yet.

And you know what? That's okay. Actually, it's even better than that. Because if I had made it back then, I never would have had a chance to go on this amazing journey. I loved those days back in school when I was staying up all night finishing up my next song and then had to go to class in the morning on no sleep. I have an amazing life today, and I'm grateful that I get to share my music with the world, but I miss those days now. There were so many times when I went days without getting a real night's sleep. But I loved being able to say to myself, *Shit, man, I didn't sleep this week, but I really grinded.*

That's the level of dedication that it takes to succeed, and I mean to *really* succeed, at the highest level. You have to be so into what you're doing that you literally have to force yourself to take a break, because otherwise you'll physically harm yourself. This may sound extreme, and that's because it is. But listen, becoming the best at something is pretty extreme, too.

If being the best is really what you want, you have to be realistic about the journey you'll have to go on to get there. But don't forget to have fun on that journey, too. I love making music and always have, to the point of obsession. There's (almost) nothing I'd rather be doing, so it doesn't feel like a sacrifice at all for me to dedicate all of my time and energy to my music. It's easy to work hard at the things you love to do, because it doesn't really feel like work at all.

>> It's easy to work hard at the things you love to do, because it doesn't really feel like work at all.

If there's something that you're already obsessed with that you want to spend all of your time becoming the best at, that's great. If not, you have to make a decision. You can be a floating leaf all your life and hope that you eventually land on something you enjoy, or you can choose what you want to dedicate your life to. People have become successful and broken into industries at all ages, but the sooner you choose, the better your shot of success. You'll simply have more time to perfect your skills. Again, it's just math.

I'm not saying that you should stop reading here, but the absolute best advice that I can give you is to decide what you want most in life and then go after it with all of your might. It's as simple as that.

Most people think that you have to be passionate about whatever you choose to focus on, but in reality, that's not true at all. You don't even really have to like it. Focusing on something you enjoy or you're passionate about is not a requirement. It's just for your comfort. The truth is, you can work hard at anything. It's just harder to stay disciplined the less passionate you are.

Loving music made it easier for me to put so many hours into it, but there are days when it doesn't come so easy, and I still have to find the motivation to grind just as hard. Like I said, I had to rewrite the hook for "Savage Love" eight times before I got it right. Sweating it out in my studio, I felt anything but passionate, but my hard work still paid off.

With that being said, if passion doesn't drive you, then you have to find something that does. Otherwise, you'll never be motivated to keep going through all the setbacks and tough times that are an inevitable part of the process. It doesn't really matter what drives you, though. Just find something.

Maybe you want to be famous and make your family proud. Maybe you want a fat checkbook. Maybe you want to represent your people on a massive scale. Or maybe you feel that you're working on something that's connected to a deeper spiritual purpose. That's nice, but again, it's not necessary, and anyone who says otherwise is fooling themselves.

Just look at me. Back in middle school, I saw the girls on the track team, and I was like, *Yo, why aren't I running track?* I wasn't a naturally fast runner, and I for sure wasn't passionate about it, but I was motivated by the idea of being around those girls. I ran my butt off, and I got pretty good. LOL.

Even today, I'm not driven at the gym because I find some deeper meaning in lifting. Naw, y'all, it's because I want the end result. I want that pot of gold at the end of the rainbow, which is a healthy mind, body, and spirit. And of course looking decent isn't the worst bonus in the world. Likewise, let whatever gets you through the journey be your driving force.

When I started getting active on social media, I was driven by nothing more than plain old fun. Fun was something that we all needed more of during the pandemic, and at the time it was enough to drive me. I loved the fact that I could post whatever I wanted on TikTok for no better reason than the fact that I was feeling it that day. On TikTok, I could be as inventive as I wanted to be. It quickly became another creative outlet that I enjoyed almost as much as I loved writing music.

In fact, the process is weirdly similar in a lot of ways. When I sit down to think about what sort of video I want to make, I have free creative rein. I get to come up with the concept, the look of the video, the background music, and how it all comes together. It's the same thing when I write a song. Once I have a concept in mind, I have to choose the kick drum, the snare, the melody, and the lyrics. It's like fitting together the pieces of a puzzle, and that process is fun as hell for me.

However, fun does not always mean easy. It takes a lot of hours and a lot of energy to create something fun. The same thing is true of influencers on social media. There is no such thing as being "famous for being famous" or being "famous for no reason." The number of times those kinds of comments are thrown around is crazy to me. It is easy for people to dismiss hard work and intention when something is presented to them as casual, easy, fun viewing.

The most successful influencers I know put in the hours, just like the most successful people in every industry. And when I got serious about social media, I knew that was what I had to do, too. One such influencer, Charli D'Amelio, told me that she posted at least two videos on TikTok every single day. Another influencer I'd gotten to know, Addison Rae, told me that she posted six. Since I was just starting to build my audience, I set a goal to post six videos a day, too. It took up a lot of my time and energy. But I was loving it. I was obsessed. So it never felt like a burden at all.

I wasn't driven to post on TikTok by the prospect of making money, but it's okay if money is what drives you. In fact, if you're driven enough by anything, money will most likely end up being a by-product of your success. On TikTok, I was leading with love and trying to brighten people's days, and because of the work I put in, it eventually became the source of some of my biggest business. I didn't go in intending to make millions of dollars on a social media app, but that's where I ended up. And I ain't mad at it at all.

It doesn't matter what drives you as long as something does. Think about what you really want in this life with no judgment and no shame. You can't fake it. You'll only put in the crazy amount of work that it takes to succeed if you want it badly enough, not if you're forcing yourself to be driven by what sounds good or what somebody else wants for you. That drive is the engine that's going to get you through your journey. Give yourself enough power to enjoy it as much as I've loved every minute of mine.

14

WORK HARDEST AT WHAT COMES EASIEST.

« »

GO FROM GOOD TO GREAT.

After working my butt off and training with Frank, I not only made my high school basketball team my sophomore year, but I became a starter on the nationally ranked varsity team. My junior year at Dillard High School, our team was ranked in the top twenty in the country. My life became split between basketball and music. It wasn't exactly fifty-fifty, but there was definitely a divide.

The basketball games at Dillard were lit. We played on a college court that was bigger than a typical high school one—roughly the same length as what you see in the NBA. At every game, the bleachers were full, and the crowd was hyped. There were cheerleaders, lights, music, signs, the whole nine.

Whenever we traveled to play against other teams at their spot, it felt weak in comparison. It was like performing at the Apollo and then going back to a local South Florida competition. Our team was used to a bigger stage.

It was exciting to be on the team and to be seen as the man at school. It was what I'd always wanted, and there were plenty of perks, but there was a downside, too. By then, I was used to performing music in front of large crowds, but I was nervous about playing ball in a packed arena with screaming, cheering fans. Before each and every game, I was terrified. My digestive system went nuts, and I found it hard to give my all to the game because I was so scared. I don't think I ever made a free throw in my entire high school career. There was too much pressure. What if I missed?

All of my hard work had turned me into a good player, maybe even a great player. But I knew deep down that I wasn't the greatest player out there. And I've never in my life been satisfied with being second best.

Funny thing is, the people around me thought that I already had it on the court. My coach believed that I could go pro, mostly because of my work ethic and my mindset. No surprise, I was the kid who was always showing up early to practice and staying late after to get in a few more drills. I came in first in every running drill, in every sprinting drill, in anything that had to do with mental toughness instead of natural talent. I was a hustler, and my coach appreciated the fact that I put in work that was on a different level than anybody else.

I loved basketball, and I never minded doing all that work because I enjoyed the game. Plus, it always feels good to see yourself improving at something. It was the same with music, and I worked just as hard on it, but I had started earlier in life. By then, I had already racked up years of obsessive practice: hundreds of sleepless nights and early mornings working at my craft. It's hard to re-create that same energy for an entirely different discipline. If basketball had been my first love, I would have gone after it with every ounce of me, and I would have succeeded because of my mindset. But I wanted to keep working just as hard at my music so I could keep improving at that even more.

The problem was, and always will be, that there are only so many hours in the day. When I left for school in the morning, the sun hadn't come up yet, and when I got home at night, it was already back down. Then there were the games themselves, which often required me to take another long bus ride to and from a competing school. After all that, I still stayed up late at night working on my music. I loved the grind, but I also knew deep down that this routine wasn't sustainable in the long term.

Even if I could have somehow kept up that pace, I knew that I was improving at both basketball and music more slowly because I was splitting my time between the two. Again, it all comes down to math. Any number of hours is greater when it's focused on one thing than it is when it's divided by two (or more). And as I said, getting better at anything is all about the number of hours that you put into it, as long as you're giving each hour your all.

Frank is the one who finally came to me and asked me the hard question that I'd been avoiding asking myself: "Is it gonna be music or is it gonna be basketball?"

It was a tough decision. Frank had helped me become the basketball player that I was. I never would have made the team without him. We had worked so hard together, and I was finally becoming the kind of player that I had always wanted to be. This was something I'd been dreaming of for years. But music was my obsession. I had to face the fact that I couldn't be a pro basketball player *and* a world-class musician. I had to choose.

I won't drag this part out, because you already know what happened. After all, you've never heard my name at the top of an NBA game, have you?

At the end of the day, I love basketball, but I'm obsessed with music. That's the difference. Plus, because of those years of hard work, music came more naturally to me. With basketball, I knew that I would always have to put in the extra effort to keep up with the pack.

After my junior year, I quit the basketball team to focus 100 percent on my music.

In a way, playing basketball reaffirmed the fact that I was born to be a singer. I knew that no one would ever be able to touch me on a stage or in the studio—especially if I applied all of myself to music instead of splitting that effort between music and the court.

Had I stuck with basketball, I have no doubt that I could have played in college. Who knows, maybe I even would have ended up going pro. But I consciously chose to become a global superstar instead, and I have no regrets.

As I said, you don't have to focus your efforts on something you love or enjoy, what the world expects of you, an area that you feel is connected to your higher purpose, or one that's guaranteed to make you rich. These things might make it easier for you to fully commit yourself and put in the massive amount of work that's required. That's important. But they're not necessary for you to succeed.

If you want to make it big, you can focus on whatever you want, and that's the truth. But you do need to focus. Pick *one* thing that you're going to focus all of your time and energy on. Pick it as soon as you can. And if you want the best possible chance of success, make it the thing that comes the most naturally to you.

>> Pick *one* thing that you're going to focus all of your time and energy on. Pick it as soon as you can. And if you want the best possible chance of success, make it the thing that comes the most naturally to you.

Sure, you can still learn other skills and enjoy other outlets, but give them just enough time and energy to get what you want out of them. Save the rest for the one area where it will be the easiest for you to go from good to great.

It's wild to me how many people do the exact opposite of this. They work the hardest on the things they're not so great at and lean on their existing skills to coast on the things that come easiest to them. Either that, or they just try a little bit of everything and spread themselves too thin. But no one is truly the best in the world at more than one completely unrelated thing. I never really believed that I could be a world-class athlete *and* a pop superstar. But I knew that I could be one or the other, depending on how much I was willing to hustle and grind.

If I'd continued to divide my time instead of choosing music back then, there's no way I would have the career that I do today. The same thing goes for everyone who's out there killing it in their chosen field. The most direct formula for success is to start out ahead, focus 100 percent, and keep on putting in the work. That's how you get ahead of the pack and stay there, because in this world, it's not enough to merely keep up.

I'll give you another example, and it's related to basketball in a way, because improving so much at hoops taught me how to use my mindset to become better at something completely physical. I did this again four years later when I broke into pop music and had to turn myself into a great dancer. Dancing had always been a side skill for me, while singing and writing music were—and are—my focus and my heart.

With that being said, I thought I was a pretty good dancer when I was first starting out in this business. Back in Florida, I could do some dope moves compared to the dancers I'd trained with. I already had a solid base, and then at AMDA, I improved my skills even more by learning all kinds of dance in addition to hip-hop, like jazz, tap, and even ballet.

Before my first album came out, I took a hip-hop class just to brush up on my skills—or so I thought. Looking at myself in the full-length mirror side by side with the other dancers, I realized that they were on a whole other level. They were *in it* with dance the same way I was all-in on my music. They fucking loved it and worked their asses off at it, and as a result they were incredible.

I see the same thing now in all of the amazing dancers I work with in my live shows and in my videos. For them, an eight-hour dance rehearsal is fun. I can make it through those eight hours, too. But at a certain point, my eyes glaze over—probably the same way theirs would glaze over in an eight-hour studio session while I'm having the time of my life.

Still, I knew that I had to be a good dancer in order to put on the kind of stage show I'd always imagined, so I worked hard at getting better. I developed a strict routine that included taking a dance class three times each week. And my skills improved. But I always make sure to keep focusing on music no matter what else I'm working on or is going on around me.

Once your career starts popping, exciting opportunities start getting thrown your way, and you get pulled in a million different directions. I'm not saying that you shouldn't take advantage of all that and enjoy the fruits of your labor. But if you want your career to last, you've got to remember what made you successful in the first place.

While one artist is partying, going to events, and celebrating their success, tons of young up-and-comers are living in their studios doing nothing but making content. They're working on their craft all night long, gaining on the artist who's hot today but might end up being gone tomorrow.

This is one reason you see a lot of artists suffer from a "sophomore slump." They spend their whole lives grinding on that first album or movie or book or whatever it is that they do. Then they lose focus just when it's time to create a follow-up that hits the same bar as the first.

I never went through this because I always stayed focused on how I could get to the next level in my career. After my first album blew up, I didn't get a big head or sit back feeling great about myself. I knew that just having some hot songs today gave me no guarantees about tomorrow. To hold on to that success, I had to adopt a marathon mindset and refuse to give up or lose focus, even for one day.

In the back of my mind, I was always thinking about how I could compete with some young kid out there who was writing a dozen songs every day the same way I used to. Basically, I had to compete with the younger, hungrier version of myself. I could only compete by actually still being him and putting in the same amount of work that he did.

>> In the back of my mind, I was always thinking about how I could compete with some young kid out there who was writing a dozen songs every day the same way I used to.

Now, I'm keenly aware of the fact that there's always more for me to learn and grow. Despite my success, I am at the peak of wanting to know more about my craft. And every day that I wake up, I'm still chasing the next dream.

I spend every day asking myself how I can best myself. I give myself small goals that I make sure to accomplish. This way, I get used to the feeling of winning, which wires my mind to achieve.

If you don't program your own mindset like this, your mind will program it for you. Most likely, you'll get stuck in default mode, thinking, *Aight, we chilling today.* Instead of letting this happen, I make sure that every goal I meet solidifies my mindset of working, winning, and accomplishing exactly what I set out to do.

>> Most likely, you'll get stuck in default mode, thinking, *Aight, we chilling today.* Instead of letting this happen, I make sure that every goal I meet solidifies my mindset of working, winning, and accomplishing exactly what I set out to do.

This mindset helps me continue focusing on my music even when there are flashier opportunities out there. When I do take one of those opportunities, I stick to my plan of putting in just enough to get what I need out of it.

One example is the time I spent guest judging on TV talent competitions, most notably *So You Think You Can Dance*. I really enjoyed doing those live shows, and I learned a lot from them about how to speak in front of an audience. As a singer, I had gotten used to doing interviews about my music and talking about my songs, but that was about it. I never had to speak to a crowd in a way that kept their attention and sounded compelling and informed.

I viewed the experience on this show as a way for me to improve on those skills. But since then, I've turned down a slew of offers to appear on similar shows. I had already extracted what I needed from this experience, so it was more beneficial for me to spend that time focusing on my music.

I approach social media the same way. TikTok is now a big source of business for me, but I'm still mindful of never letting it cannibalize my music career. In order to meet my goals, these two things have to support each other instead of ever taking away from each other.

I don't have an exact formula, but I always try to focus my time and energy on the area where they're most needed at that moment. Sometimes it's time to conceive and post a new TikTok video, and sometimes it's music time. But even when it's not music time, I make sure to work on music for at least a couple of hours every day. It's like going to the gym for me. To compete at my level and stay in tip-top shape, I've got to keep those muscles strong.

I'll say it again: Success does not happen by accident. Greatness does not happen by accident. And neither of them happens quickly or conveniently, either. These are just facts, and it doesn't help anything to pretend they're not true. Making it at a high level is going to require your all—your focus, your dedication, your energy, and your time.

>> I'll say it again: Success does not happen by accident.

You want to be a jack-or-jill-of-all-trades? More power to you. But that's not how you achieve big-time success. To have that kind of success, you have to be the greatest in the world at the one thing that you choose to spend your life pursuing. And the simple fact is that it's easier to become the great*est* when you give 100 percent of yourself in an area where you're already great.

15

CHOOSE YOUR
COMPETITION.

« »

AND KEEP PUSHING
THAT BAR HIGHER.

On the edge of discomfort comes growth.
Put in the work and push on the edges,
get uncomfortable, and grow.

—DANNY WHITE, ENTREPRENEUR

As you know, Frank had played pro basketball in Europe, and his younger brother, Hakeem, also had skills. When we met, he wanted to go pro just as Frank had, and with Hakeem's natural talent, I had no doubt that this goal was within his reach.

The three of us used to spend a lot of time playing basketball together. Other times, I played with Hakeem. Most of the time, Hakeem and I played one-on-one full court just to tire each other out.

When Frank joined us, he always beat me. Hakeem usually whooped my ass pretty good, too, but not always and often not by much.

The more we played, the more I noticed that from game to game, Hakeem's skills stayed about the same. He was naturally good, but he was relying on that natural ability instead of putting in the work to become the best in the world, or at least the best that he could possibly be.

I sat him down one day after we played and tried to preach to him. "Man, you're good," I told him. "But there's no way you and I should be competing. We shouldn't even be in the same ballpark, because I'm never going to be in the NBA."

I wasn't trying to be harsh, but I knew about his goals, and it was clear to me that if he stayed on his current path, he wasn't going to get there. "If you want to go pro, the fact that you're only *kind of* beating me is not good enough."

Hakeem was not alone. Most folks look at the other people around them and try to compete at that level. But this is just about the most limiting thing that you can do. After all, how many of the people you know are going to make it on a massive scale? The reality is that being the very best at your school or in your town or on your team or on whatever field you're currently playing on has absolutely no bearing on whether or not you'll have any real and lasting success.

If you want to succeed in the real world—and I mean *really* succeed—you've got to be able to go toe to toe with the best on the planet. This means that to have even a shred of a chance, you need to be light-years ahead of anyone you're competing against now.

I've seen this my entire life. Starting at a very young age, my classmates at my performing arts schools were some of the most talented kids in South Florida. A lot of them competed against one another to get the chorus solo or to be chosen as the first-chair violinist in the orchestra or to land the lead in the school play or whatnot.

I never wasted one minute of my time or one spark of my energy worrying about beating those kids. Even then, I knew that I wasn't really competing against them. I didn't even feel as though I was competing against the ones I went up against in the local talent shows.

Again, no disrespect. Most of those kids were good. Some of them were great. But how many of them were selling millions of records? It didn't matter whether I beat those kids or not. I always had my eye on the real competition: the best artists in the world. What mattered was whether or not I could beat *them*.

As I said, my classmates were the best *in South Florida,* but I didn't want to be the best in South Florida. I wanted to be, again, *the best in the world.* To get there, I knew that I had to think much bigger than just trying to beat the kids who happened to be in class with me.

This meant that from day one, I was looking at Michael Jackson and thinking about how I could get to *that* level. I was watching B2K and wondering how I could beat *them*. I was studying Justin Timberlake's sales numbers and asking myself how I could sell records like *that*.

I wanted to be good enough to compete against the artists who were making a real impact and touching people around the globe. I knew that working hard enough to compete against those folks was the only way for me to succeed on a massive scale. And even if I never reached that level and landed right below them, I would still have a chance to impact the world in a positive way.

If we're looking at pure statistics, the truth is that most likely the people around you won't make it to the top 1 percent. If that's not your goal, that's cool. I just want to state the hard facts. You can never forget that there is a whole big world out there full of people who have the same interests as you, share the same passions as you, and who want to succeed and dominate in the same fields as you. Those are the people you're competing against, not the guy next door or the star player on your team or even the boss at your job. Start comparing yourself to the greatest of all time, not just the greatest in *your* area at *your* time.

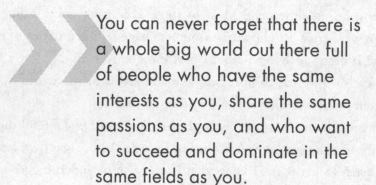

> You can never forget that there is a whole big world out there full of people who have the same interests as you, share the same passions as you, and who want to succeed and dominate in the same fields as you.

If you set your bar to match or to just beat your local talent, you'll either improve a little bit or you'll maintain the same skill level that you have right now. That's fine, but riding a plateau will never get you to the top of the mountain. Comparing yourself to some of the greatest, instead, will keep you hungry and grabbing for that next summit until you reach it. Then you'll start grabbing for the next one after that. If you shoot for the 1 percent and make it to the top 10, you're still giving yourself a chance to make an impact.

As you travel upward, you're going to fail sometimes. We already know that. You're also going to lose. And just as it's okay to fail in the short term as long as you succeed in the long term, losing small battles won't hold you back, either, if you keep your eyes on the bigger prize. It would be nice to win every competition on the road to success, but it isn't necessary. And sometimes, you'll look back and realize that those losses were really long-term wins.

For me, this meant never getting past the first table at the auditions for *American Idol*.

I was fifteen years old in the early 2000s, and *American Idol* was the biggest show on TV. I'd been winning local singing competitions for years, and I felt that this audition was the obvious next step. My mom took the day off work to drive me to some location I can't even remember. It was hours away from our home. We got out of the car at an enormous warehouse that took up an entire block and found a line of people wrapped around the whole warehouse and even farther down the street. I had expected there to be a lot of people there, but . . . damn.

My mom and I waited in that line all day. I'm talking about ten hours at least. We took turns leaving the line to get food or to go to the bathroom. Finally, I left my mom waiting outside and entered the enormous warehouse, which was one giant open room. Not the best acoustics in the world. There were literally hundreds of tables in the room with a judge sitting at each one. Not a Simon Cowell type of judge, either—someone from behind the scenes.

Meanwhile, there were aspiring singers auditioning at every table. That's a thousand people singing all different songs at one time. Above the singing, I could hear the chorus of judges saying, "Next . . . next . . . next . . ."

I took a breath and approached one of the tables. I knew how slim my chances were, but I was still feeling confident. As usual, I had "borrowed" an outfit from Joey—a tight-fitting sleeveless T, some fake chains, and baggy, ripped jeans. But it didn't matter what I was wearing because the judge barely looked at me. She just nodded quickly.

This was one of the most nerve-wracking experiences of my life. I wanted it so bad. I was shaking and my throat was dry, but I started to sing "Love" by Musiq Soulchild. There was no music. You don't get music at a cattle call. And I was so nervous that I started in a key that was too low for me. I was exactly seven seconds into the song when the woman cut me off. "Thank you very much," she called out loudly. "NEEEEEXXT."

After a whole day of waiting, I felt I hadn't gotten a fair chance, and I knew I hadn't done my best. But when my mom asked me how it went, I lied and told her I did okay. I was too embarrassed to admit the truth, that I had choked.

I lost that day, and it definitely bruised my ego. But now I realize that winning would not have been good for my career in the long run. The truth is that shows like *American Idol* are more about the judges, the spectacle, and the ratings than they are about launching artists' careers. Sometimes the losses are really wins in the bigger picture. Never forget that or let the misses keep you from shooting your next shot.

Plus, the thousands of people auditioning that day were not my real competition.

Likewise, your competition is the top dogs. Focus on winning against *them*.

Setting the bar that high—which may seem impossibly high—is essential to making it in the creative world, the music world, the comedy world, the business world, you name it. You can't be sleeping on the job, because there are so many other people out there who are wide-awake and are more than willing and ready to pass you by.

 You can't be sleeping on the job, because there are so many other people out there who are wide-awake and are more than willing and ready to pass you by.

The other thing I learned from losing at the *American Idol* audition: you have to impress immediately and go for the gusto from the start, no matter what you're doing. You can't take the time to work your way in. The song "Love" builds fairly quickly, but I should have chosen a song that showed my vocal ability immediately, from the very first second.

This is exactly how it is today on social media. Not only do you have to grab people's attention right out the gate, but the competition is stiffer than ever, too. These days, it's not even enough to be able to compete with the best of the best in your specific genre or in your chosen field. Musical artists used to be able to succeed by being "just" the best pop singer or the best country singer. They were still up against the best in the world, but that pool of competition was so much smaller.

Now, with the way we consume content changing so fast and with all of us spending more and more time on our phones, music is competing for people's attention against every other form of content out there. People aren't just choosing between pop songs. They're choosing between every type of song, every movie, every TV show, every YouTube video, and every social media post, all at the same time.

This means that as a singer, it's not enough to be "just" as good as Ariana Grande or Justin Bieber. And as an actor, it's not enough to be "only" as good as Meryl Streep or Leonardo DiCaprio. On and on in every field. It might seem to be setting too high of a bar to strive to be as good as *any one* of these people. But it would still be a whole lot easier than facing the massive amount of competition we're all up against now in *every* field. I'm telling you, it's no joke. And I wouldn't be doing you any favors if I didn't give it to you straight.

So who are the heroes that you'd love to be able to compare yourself to one day? If you don't already know, that's cool. Take a moment to think about it right now. Maybe even write down a list. Which people do you look up to, and why? Who inspires you, and why? Who is making the kind of impact on the world that you would like to emulate, and why?

Now be real with yourself for a minute. How do your talents, your skills, and your creative output stack up against your heroes' abilities? Are you really ready to play on the same field as them? Think about how much work they put in to get to where they are. That's *bare minimum* for you.

Once you know who inspires you, study those people. Don't just compete against them. Draw from them, too. No great artist has ever existed in a vacuum. Use what you learn from the best out there to create a blueprint for yourself.

I've been drawing from greatness my whole life, and I used that to create a blueprint for my art when I was just a few years old. Michael Jackson was the sole reason that I started singing and dancing to begin with. He was everything that I wanted to become from a musical standpoint, a philanthropic perspective, and in terms of his global impact. Before I was in kindergarten, I was in front of the TV trying to do the moonwalk in my socks like every other kid. But I wasn't like them other kids. I wasn't just a fan. For me, it was a full-blown obsession.

I didn't just admire Michael; I wanted to *be* him. I sang like Michael for so many years that my vocal timbre still comes out sounding derivative. I haven't tried to sound like him in decades, but you can still hear his influence in my voice because I spent so long training myself to sing like him. I've also drawn from his choreography, with its elevated, clean lines that are a real departure from typical hip-hop dances.

Michael was also the king of the 1980s, and that era of music has inspired my songwriting more than any other. So many of the best artists in the 1980s were disciples of Michael. It's impossible to avoid his influence if you draw from any pop singer of that era.

When I wrote "Want to Want Me" in 2015, I set out to create an epic, fun dance song that could hold its own against some of the most well-known and loved songs of the 1980s. As I was working on the song, I was loving it. It was upbeat, infectious, and sexy without being raunchy. It was also one of those songs that came pretty easily, with the help of some of my favorite collaborators. After we recorded the song, I felt confident that we had made another hit.

But I always say that the real test of any song is the overnight run. Sometimes, when I listen to a song the next day, it hits different. This time, for some reason that I couldn't quite put my finger on, it didn't feel like me. I figured that maybe it wasn't as good as I'd thought.

Instead of scrapping the song, though, I sent it to a bunch of people whose opinions I respected. I didn't get any of those, "Yeah, this is cool," responses. Naw, everyone was flipping out and saying it was incredible. I took this feedback seriously, but I still wasn't convinced. "I don't know about this one," I said to Frank. "I'm not sure if it's me."

"You're tripping," he told me. "This is the one."

For more than a decade at that point, Frank had been helping me make these kinds of decisions, and I respected his opinions almost as much as I trusted my own. So we decided to release "Want to Want Me" as the lead single of my fourth album. It quickly became a top-five hit in the US and took the number one spot in many countries around the world.

Here's the truth: I was wrong. My gut is usually right about my songs, but I admit wholeheartedly that I had the wrong perspective on "Want to Want Me." (This is another example of why it's so important to have the right bees in your hive.)

I knew it had to be a good song if it was such a big hit. As always, the numbers don't lie. But I really started to come around on "Want to Want Me" when I performed it live. To this day, audiences go wild, dancing and singing along whenever I perform that song, and I feed off that reaction from the crowd. This made it eventually go from a song that I wasn't really about at first to my absolute favorite song to perform.

Now I realize that I had set out to write an epic, 1980s-style dance song, and that's exactly what I had done. I didn't feel the magic in the recording because it's a song that's meant to be sung and enjoyed and danced to live—with the kind of performance and choreography that's a part of my Michael Jackson blueprint.

Once you have your blueprint, though, that's where it ends. I'm not talking about straight up copying other people. The next step is to find yourself within that blueprint. The beauty in all art is the creativity that is unique to the person that created it.

Plus, I've learned the hard way that it's way easier to be yourself than it is to try to copy someone else. (Spiked leather jacket, anyone?) It's just not interesting to see a replica of another successful person. To succeed, you've got to create something that nobody has ever seen or heard before. Go ahead and draw from your heroes, but always make sure to put your own spin on whatever you create. Otherwise, there's no point in creating it at all.

Over time, this happened naturally for me. My metric for creating something original is to make sure the songs that I sing sound good coming from my voice and no one else's. The choreography I use has to look good on my body and no one else's. And conceptually, I build on whatever happens to intrigue me personally in that moment.

If I find a cool, unique sound, I'll write a song around it, period. If it sounds crazy and different and as though only I could have written it? Perfect. I believe that this type of experimentation has played a big role in my longevity as an artist, because my stuff is never boring. As soon as you think you've got me all figured out, I go and do something completely different. Case in point: a lot of critics commented that "Want to Want Me" had far more of an '80s sound than my previous songs. That shift kept people guessing, in a good way.

Being from the islands also helps me put my own stamp on my music. I may be all-American when it comes to my tastes in movies, sports, and hamburgers, but my Haitian culture has heavily influenced me as both an artist and as a person. Sometimes my accent comes out of nowhere, both when I'm singing and talking (especially after I've had a couple drinks). I also incorporate a lot of Haitian compas sounds into my music. And of course, my choreography has to complement those island rhythms, too.

I never want to lose my sense of inspiration, though. To aspire to greatness, I keep my eyes on greatness. The first floor of my house is filled with portraits of some of the artists and heroes that I've drawn inspiration from over the years.

One of those people is Muhammad Ali. When he was talking about sit-ups, Ali once said, "I only start counting when it starts hurting because those are the only ones that count." I repeat those words to myself whenever I'm facing a challenge, whether it's at the gym or the studio or life in general. It's the work you put in after it gets tough and everyone else has quit that makes all the difference.

Just recently, I was rehearsing for some upcoming shows. Since the beginning of the pandemic, I hadn't been performing as much as I used to. I was trying to get back into it and become the same performer that I was before, but it was a bit of a struggle to get there.

One night, we had an eight-hour rehearsal, and I was tired as shit. We took a break at the halfway point. In this case, halfway meant we'd already been at it for four hours. As I chugged some water, I asked myself how I could possibly make it through another four. For a moment, I allowed myself to think about all the artists who would have gone home at that point and allowed the dancers to finish the rehearsal themselves. It was tempting. But even as this thought crossed my mind, I knew that wasn't me.

I forced myself to stay and give my all for the entire rehearsal. It was brutal, but afterward, I was so glad that I had stuck it out. The shows were better as a result. It's those moments when you feel like giving up and you push through anyway that make the real difference. That's the lesson from Muhammad Ali.

My main point here is the same one that I tried to preach at Frank's brother, Hakeem, as we sat there sweating on a bench on the side of the basketball court: *You have to decide exactly what you want in life. Then give it everything you've got. If you work harder than anyone else, you can live the life you want. With the right mindset, you can achieve any goal, no matter how lofty.*

Most people don't realize that they even have a choice about who they will become and the life that they will live, but the fact is that it's entirely up to you. Isn't that incredible? Based on what you choose, you'll have one of two totally different lives. If you go HAM today to wipe out even the toughest competition, the whole world will open up to you. You'll find an amazing life that you can control.

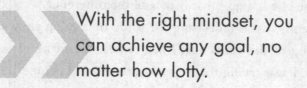

> With the right mindset, you can achieve any goal, no matter how lofty.

I'm not by any means saying that you'll have a bad or somehow inferior life if you don't choose to put that kind of work in, but it's a fact that your life *will* be different. You can coast and become the best in your town, and that will be your legacy. There's nothing wrong with that at all—as long as it's what you truly want.

No one else can choose your legacy for you. You have the chance to decide for yourself who you want to be.

Nobody ever became world-class without superhuman levels of work and dedication. I sure as hell didn't, and neither will you. But I honestly don't think it's out of your reach, either. Nothing in this world really is.

THE RULES AT A GLANCE

1. TAKE RISKS

2. UNLOCK CLOSED DOORS

3. YOU ARE ONLY AS GOOD AS YOUR ROUTINE

4. SUCCESS IS FOR RENT

5. STOP SHOWING OFF

6. OBSTACLES ARE OPPORTUNITIES

7. DECIDE WHAT IS IMPORTANT TO YOU

8. THOSE WHO CAN, DO

9. RESPECT THE HIVE

10. TRUST THE DATA

11. COLLABORATE, PERIOD

12. REVEAL YOURSELF IN YOUR BEST LIGHT

13. TALENT IS OVERRATED

14. WORK HARDEST AT WHAT COMES EASIEST

15. CHOOSE YOUR COMPETITION

ACKNOWLEDGMENTS

I spoke earlier about the power of collaboration. Throughout my career, I have had the privilege of working with some of the best of the best in music, in business, and most recently, in writing this book. I am grateful for every individual I have had the opportunity to collaborate with. As I said earlier, "No one is an island, nor should they be."

Thank you to Dan Milaschewski and the whole team at UTA; to my editor, Sydney Rogers, for your unwavering vision and commitment to this book; and to my publisher, Judith Curr, for all of your support. Also at HarperCollins, thank you to Stephen Brayda, Aly Mostel, Melinda Mullin, and the global HarperCollins publishing team who saw the value of *Sing Your Name Out Loud* for readers around the world. Thank you to my collaborator Jodi Lipper, who took my advice, my story, and my words, and made them sing.

Outside of the publishing world, thank you to my business partner Danny White for helping me see which risks are worth taking, to Frank Harris for all of your wisdom and mentorship throughout the years, and to Harry Dessources for being there with me every day from the beginning. A huge thank you to Ellen DeGeneres, Drew Taggart and Alex Pall, Luke Bryan, Zedd, David Guetta, Will Smith, and Tyler Hubbard and Brian Kelley for sharing your words of wisdom.

And most of all, thank you to my fans, my readers, and my followers for singing along with me, dancing along with me, laughing along with me, and crying along with me. Thank you for taking this journey with me. Now it's your turn to *Sing Your Name Out Loud*.

ABOUT THE AUTHOR

JASON DERULO is a global superstar whose music and personality transcend borders, generations, and genres. Since his debut single reached number one in 2009, Jason has gone on to sell well over 250 million singles worldwide and to earn twelve billion global streams. In 2020, with the viral sensation "Savage Love," Derulo joined the exclusive list of artists with a number one song in three consecutive decades. *Sing Your Name Out Loud* is his first book.